Crochet Zodiac Dolls

Stitch the horoscope with
astrological amigurumi

CARLA MITRANI

DAVID & CHARLES

www.davidandcharles.com

Crochet Zodiac Dolls

Contents

Introduction

Ever since we walked the face of the Earth, we have gazed at the skies in wonder: the Sun, the Moon, the stars and the planets have always been there to give us answers. Through Astrology we have tried to understand how their movements and combinations affected our lives. Rulers, kings and queens of yore, medieval writers and poets, consulted the skies before making any important decisions.

Like those before us, I also like to believe that much of who we are is written in the stars and that they can offer answers as to why we act as we do why we can't fully explain it. If you, like me, have ever wondered why you or someone you know acts in a certain way, or why you get on so well with your best friend, then this book is for you, and we will have a lot of fun together!

Here you will find a doll to depict each Sun sign of the Zodiac, a brief description of their personality traits, lucky colour and gemstone, and matching compatibilities. Use these patterns to crochet a doll for that special Pisces friend who always has your back, or that amazing Taurus teacher, or that adventurous Sagittarius cousin of yours. Pair the dolls with a book describing their Zodiac sign, or with their lucky stone or even get their birth charts done!

Just have fun and let the stars, planets and hooks guide your way!

Zodiac Sign	Depiction	Element	Ruling Planet	Best Character Trait	Lucky Colour	Lucky Gemstone
Aries	The Ram	Fire	Mars	Courage	Red	Diamond
Taurus	The Bull	Earth	Venus	Strength	Green	Emerald
Gemini	The Twins	Air	Mercury	Adaptability	Yellow	Citrine
Cancer	The Crab	Water	Moon	Compassion	Silver	Moonstone
Leo	The Lion	Fire	Sun	Generosity	Orange	Ruby
Virgo	The Maiden	Earth	Mercury	Organization	Blue	Blue Sapphire
Libra	The Scales	Air	Venus	Fairness	Blue	Opal
Scorpio	The Scorpion	Water	Pluto	Willpower	Burgundy	Topaz
Sagittarius	The Archer	Fire	Jupiter	Enthusiasm	Purple	Turquoise
Capricorn	The Sea Goat	Earth	Saturn	Determination	Brown	Garnet
Aquarius	The Water-bearer	Air	Uranus	Ingenuity	Blue	Purple Amethyst
Pisces	The Two Fish	Water	Neptune	Empathy	Turquoise	Aquamarine

The Wheel of Life

The Zodiac represents one full circle of the Sun and during that journey it passes through 12 different zones. The Sun stays approximately one month in each zone. Since the Sun is the most influential celestial object of the horoscope, your sign is determined by the zone it occupied on the day you were born—this influences your character, your personal qualities and your talents. The entire year-long journey of the Sun begins at the Spring equinox, when it enters the sign of Aries (energetic and daring) and finishes in Pisces (a true release force).

The Wheel of Life shows all the signs together as they present themselves during the year, but it also shows the attraction of the opposing signs, known as polarities. Use the wheel to find your opposite sign. Opposing signs often work successfully in a beautiful balancing act, just like life itself—a constant exercise in equilibrium.

Elements

Personality is affected by the 12 distinct Zodiac signs, but signs are also connected to the four elements, each of which have their own characteristics. The four astrology elements are fire, earth, air and water and each of the 12 Zodiac signs falls into one of these four elements. Once you know which element rules your sign, you can better understand your nature.

FIRE

The fire signs are Aries, Leo and Sagittarius and these people tend to be driven, determined, enthusiastic and active. They are usually the ones who throw themselves into a project and don't give up until it's finished.

EARTH

The earth signs are Taurus, Virgo and Capricorn and they are known for being practical, grounded, determined and cautious. The dependable nature of people born under the earth element means they are often seen as being organised and stable.

AIR

The three air signs are Gemini, Libra and Aquarius. These people tend to feel confident in themselves and like to gather all the information before making decisions. As a result, they are generally flexible, versatile and open-minded people.

WATER

The three water signs are Cancer, Scorpio and Pisces. People born under these signs are especially adaptable to change and act according to feeling. They are willing to take risks and try new things, often being the best people to turn to when there is a tricky problem that needs to be solved.

Fire

Leo

Sagittarius

Aries

Earth

Taurus

Virgo

Capricorn

Air

Aquarius

Libra

Water

Scorpio

Pisces

Cancer

Tools and Materials

Hooks and Yarns

All the dolls in this book were crocheted using a 2mm (US B/1) crochet hook and 8/4-ply fingering weight cotton yarn. Try to crochet as tightly as possible, so that you don't create holes when stuffing the doll.

I only use 100% cotton yarns because I like the feel and finish of cotton; it runs smoothly in your hands when working and it will not pill as acrylic or woollen yarns do, which makes these dolls more durable when intended for children. Cotton also builds a sturdier fabric for stuffed dolls, which will not stretch and will hold the stuffing better, without distorting the shapes and sizes of the bodies.

CROCHET HOOKS

Size 2mm (US B/1). I really love Clover's Soft Touch hook. They have a flat handle and a tiny brown cushion for your thumb.

COTTON YARN

8/4-ply fingering weight 100% soft cotton. I worked with the following yarn by Hobbii:

8/4 RAINBOW COTTON

• Fibre: 100% soft cotton

• Ball weight: 50g (1.8oz)

• Length: 170m (186yds)

• Yarn weight: Fingering (super fine)

MOHAIR YARN

Lace weight soft and fluffy mohair yarn. For the Pisces hair I worked with the following yarn by Hobbii:

DIABLO

• Fibre: 40% acrylic, 30% mohair, 30% polyamide

• Ball weight: 2 g (0.9oz)

• Length: 225m (246yds)

• Yarn weight: lace

HOW MUCH YARN IS NEEDED?

One of the best things about making the dolls in this book is that none of them use an entire 50 g ball of yarn. In fact, you can use one ball of skin colour to make 4 dolls. So save all your leftovers and scraps, because they can become skirts, horns or accessories!

Other Tools and Materials

TOY SAFETY EYES

Plastic, black, size 6mm (¼in) are used for the dolls.

For safety reasons, if you are planning to give the doll to a small child, you should embroider the eyes using black, dark grey or brown yarn instead.

STUFFING

Polyester fibrefill stuffing – you will need to stuff firmly!

SCISSORS AND SEAM RIPPER

There are so many lovely scissors to choose from! Indulge yourself.

STITCH MARKERS

Fancy ones or… paper clips, hair pins or little pieces of yarn! But whichever you choose, do not forget to mark the beginning of each round…

TAPESTRY/YARN NEEDLE

You'll use it to sew together the different parts of your doll and for weaving in ends. Be sure to find one with a blunted tip, so it won't damage the yarn. When you find one you love, buy multiples. You just know that some will fall into unfindable places!

PINS

You'll need pins to fix certain pieces in place before sewing them. Buy those with beaded heads or plastic decorations so they don't get lost inside the doll.

WOODEN CHOPSTICK

Sushi takeaway? Ask for extra chopsticks! They are the perfect tool to squeeze the stuffing through tiny openings and spread it evenly in hard to reach places…

CRAFT BAG AND PENCIL CASE

I am the ultimate crocheter-on-the-go! When the stars align, I can be seen finishing my current WIP in the most unusual places.

Stitches

All the dolls in this book are worked in rounds, in a continuous spiral, so there's no need to close the round after finishing each one of them.

Stitch Abbreviations

The patterns in this book are written using US crochet terms. These are listed here, along with their UK equivalents (where applicable):

ch = chain stitch

slst = slip stitch

sc = single crochet (UK double crochet)

sc2tog = single crochet 2 stitches together (UK double crochet 2 stitches together)

hdc = half double crochet (UK half treble crochet)

dc = double crochet (UK treble crochet)

FLO = front loop only

BLO = back loop only

beg = beginning

rep = repeat

approx = approximately

* = denotes the beginning of a repeat sequence. Repeat the instructions that follow the * as instructed.

Stitches Used

SLIP KNOT

The slip knot is the starting point of the foundation chain and it does not count as a stitch. Make a loop shape with the tail end of the yarn. Insert the hook into it, yarn over hook and draw another loop through it. Pull the yarn tail to tighten the loop around the hook.

CHAIN STITCH (CH)

Start with a slip knot, then yarn over hook and pull through the loop on your hook to create one chain stitch. Repeat this as many times as stated in your pattern.

SLIP STITCH (SLST)

Insert your hook into the stitch, yarn over hook and pull through the stitch and the loop on the hook at the same time.

SINGLE CROCHET (SC)

Insert the hook into the stitch, yarn over hook and pull the yarn back through the stitch. You will now have two loops on the hook. Yarn over again and draw it through both loops at once.

HALF DOUBLE CROCHET (HDC)

Yarn over hook and then insert your hook into the stitch, yarn over hook and pull the yarn through the stitch (you will have three loops on the hook). Yarn over hook and pull through all three loops on the hook in one go.

DOUBLE CROCHET (DC)

Yarn over hook and insert your hook into the stitch, yarn over hook and pull the yarn through the stitch (you will have three loops on the hook). Yarn over hook and pull through the first two loops on the hook in one go (this will leave two loops remaining on the hook). Yarn over hook one last time and draw through the last two remaining loops on the hook.

SINGLE CROCHET 2 STITCHES TOGETHER (SC2TOG)

Working two stitches together creates a decrease of one stitch, and for the dolls in this book the single crochet decrease (sc2tog) is worked as an invisible decrease. See *Techniques: Invisible Single Crochet Decrease* for detailed instructions and photos.

BOBBLE STITCH (BOBBLE ST)

This is the stitch I use to create the nose of the dolls.

The bobble stitch is a cluster of unfinished dc stitches worked into one stitch, achieved by leaving the last loop of each dc on the hook and closing them all together at the end.

Work a bobble stitch by following these step-by-step instructions:

Yarn over hook (**1**) and insert the hook into the stitch. Yarn over hook again and draw the yarn through the stitch. You now have three loops on the hook (**2**). Yarn over hook again and pull it through the first two loops on the hook (**3**). You now have one unfinished double crochet stitch and two loops remain on the hook.

In the same stitch, repeat the previous steps four more times, to create four more unfinished double crochet stitches into that stitch. You must end with six loops on your hook (**4**).

Finally, yarn over hook and draw through all six loops on the hook at once, to create the cluster (**5**).

If, after finishing, you end up with the bump protruding from the wrong side of the fabric (**6**), just push it towards the outside to build the nose (**7**).

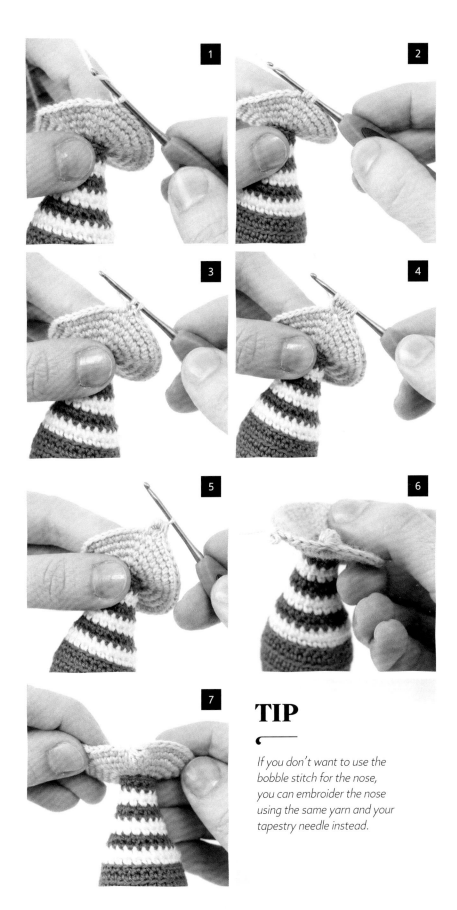

TIP

If you don't want to use the bobble stitch for the nose, you can embroider the nose using the same yarn and your tapestry needle instead.

The Projects

Yarn

100% 4-ply cotton; colours used: **skin** colour, **beige**, **white**, **dark brown**, **black**, small amount of **pink**

Hooks

Size 2mm (US B/1) hook

Other Tools and Materials

Stitch marker

Safety eyes, 2 x 6mm (¼in)

Fibrefill stuffing

Finished size

15cm (6in) tall

Aries

20 March–19 April

The 1ˢᵗ sign of the Zodiac

Here comes the first sign of the Zodiac, ready to take charge and lead the way! No obstacle is too big for brave and fearless Aries. Strong and full of vitality, like the Ram, Arians need action and know how to get things done. Friendly and outgoing, they love to share their interests and discoveries. Their energy and enthusiasm sure are contagious! So be ready, life will never be dull with an Aries by your side.

Symbol	Depiction	Element	Ruling Planet	Lucky Gemstone

Best Character Trait: Courage

Lucky Colour: Red

Notable Aries People: Leonardo da Vinci, Vincent Van Gogh, Gloria Steinem & Emma Thompson

Makes Good Friends With: Leo, Sagittarius & Aquarius

Leg 1

Round 1: Using **beige**, 6 sc in a magic ring. (6 sts)
Round 2: 2 sc in each st. (12 sts)
Round 3: 1 sc BLO in each st.
Rounds 4 to 11: 1 sc in each st.
Fasten off invisibly. Set aside.

Leg 2

Work as for Leg 1 but do not fasten off yarn. We will continue with the body.

Body

Round 12: Still with leg 2 on your hook, ch 3 and join to leg 1 with a sc in any stitch of leg 1 (*see Techniques: Joining Legs – Option 2*). Place a stitch marker on the first stitch for beg of new round. Work a further 11 sc along leg 1, 1 sc into each ch of 3-ch-loop, 12 sc all along leg 2, 1 sc into other side of each ch of 3-ch-loop. (30 sts)
Rounds 13 to 18: 1 sc in each st.
Round 19: *3 sc, sc2tog; rep from * to end. (24 sts)
Rounds 20 to 22: 1 sc in each st.
Round 23: *2 sc, sc2tog; rep from * to end. (18 sts)
Stuff the body firmly at this point.
Rounds 24 to 26: 1 sc in each st.
Round 27: *1 sc, sc2tog; rep from * to end. (12 sts)
Rounds 28 and 29: 1 sc in each st.
Round 30: Change to **skin** colour, 1 sc BLO in each st.
Round 31: 1 sc in each st.
Do not fasten off yarn. We will continue with the head.

Head

Round 32: 2 sc in each st. (24 sts)

Round 33: *1 sc, 2 sc in the next st; rep from * to end. (36 sts)

Stuff the neck area firmly at this point.

Round 34: *5 sc, 2 sc in the next st; rep from * to end. (42 sts)

We will now start crocheting the ruffled collar, as it will be easier to do so without the head in place. Place a stitch marker in the loop on your hook to secure it and cut the yarn.

Ruffled Collar

Turn the body upside down and join **white** yarn in one of the front loops of round 30, at the back of the neck.

Round 1: 2 sc in FLO of each st. (24 sts)

Round 2: 2 sc in each st. (48 sts)

Round 3: 2 sc in each st. (96 sts)

Round 4: 1 sc in each st.

Fasten off and weave in ends.

We will now continue with the head. Rejoin the **skin** colour yarn to where you stopped working the head.

Rounds 35 and 36: 1 sc in each st.

Round 37: sc in each st until you are above the middle of the legs at the front of the body, 1 bobble st for the nose (*see Stitches: Bobble st*), sc in each st to end.

Rounds 38 to 47: 1 sc in each st.

Round 48: *5 sc, sc2tog; rep from * to end. (36 sts)

Place safety eyes one round above the nose, with 8 sts between them, embroider cheeks with **pink** yarn.

Round 49: *4 sc, sc2tog; rep from * to end. (30 sts)

Round 50: *3 sc, sc2tog; rep from * to end. (24 sts)

Start stuffing the head at this point.

Round 51: *2 sc, sc2tog; rep from * to end. (18 sts)

Round 52: *1 sc, sc2tog; rep from * to end. (12 sts)

Stuff firmly.

Round 53: (sc2tog) 6 times. (6 sts)

Fasten off and weave in ends.

TIP

Arrange the collar with your fingers, giving shape to the waves up and down.

Arms (Make Two)

Round 1: Using **skin** colour, ch 2, 4 sc in the second ch from hook. (4sts)

Round 2: 2 sc in each st. (8 sts)

Rounds 3 to 5: 1 sc in each st.

Round 6: Change to **beige**, 1 sc BLO in each st.

Rounds 7 to 16: 1 sc in each st.

Round 17: Press the opening with your fingers, aligning 4 sts side by side and sc both sides together by working 1 sc into each pair of sts (*see Techniques: Closing the Arms*).

Fasten off, leaving a long tail to sew to the body.

Hood

Round 1: Using **beige**, 6 sc in a magic ring. (6 sts)

Round 2: 2 sc in each st. (12 sts)

Round 3: *1 sc, 2 sc in the next st; rep from * to end. (18 sts)

Round 4: *2 sc, 2 sc in the next st; rep from * to end. (24 sts)

Round 5: *3 sc, 2 sc in the next st; rep from * to end. (30 sts)

Round 6: *4 sc, 2 sc in the next st; rep from * to end. (36 sts)

Round 7: *5 sc, 2 sc in the next st; rep from * to end. (42 sts)

Round 8: *6 sc, 2 sc in the next st; rep from * to end. (48 sts)

Rounds 9 to 16: 1 sc in each st.

Round 17: 1 sc FLO in the next 9 sts, 1 sc in the following 31 sts, 1 sc FLO in the last 8 sts

Round 18: 1 sc in each st.

Fasten off, leaving a long tail to sew to the head.

Hair

Using **black** for the hair, attach with a slip knot in the first remaining back loop of round 17 of the hood.

Ch 11, 1 sc in the second ch from hook, 1 sc in each ch to end (10 sc), *1 slst in next back loop, ch 11, 1 sc in the second ch from hook, 1 sc in each ch to end (10 sc); rep from * to last st, 1 slst in last remaining back loop. (16 hair curls).

Fasten off, and weave in ends.

Ram Horns (Make Two)

Round 1: Using **dark brown**, ch 2, 4 sc in the second ch from hook. (4sts)

Round 2: *1 sc, 2 sc in the next st; rep from * to end. (6 sts)

Round 3: 1 sc in each st.

Round 4: *2 sc, 2 sc in the next st; rep from * to end. (8 sts)

Round 5: 1 sc BLO in each st.

Round 6: *1 sc, 2 sc in the next st; rep from * to end. (12 sts)

Round 7: 1 sc BLO in each st.

Round 8: 1 sc in each st.

Round 9: 1 sc BLO in each st.

Round 10: *3 sc, 2 sc in the next st; rep from * to end. (15 sts)

Round 11: 1 sc BLO in each st.

Round 12: 1 sc in each st.

Round 13: 1 sc BLO in each st.

Round 14: *4 sc, 2 sc in the next st; rep from * to end. (18 sts)

Round 15: 1 sc BLO in each st.

Round 16: 1 sc in each st.

Fasten off, leaving a long tail to sew to the head.

Assembly

Try the hood on the head to see how to position it. Remove it. Embroider some locks of black hair on the forehead of your doll. Sew the hood to the head (*see Techniques: Sewing the Hair*).

Sew the arms to the sides of the body (*see Techniques: Sewing the Arms*). You might need to lift the collar a bit.

Stuff the horns a little and sew them to the hood, roll the tip backwards slightly.

Using the dark brown yarn, embroider two buttons to the body of your doll.

Weave in all ends inside the doll.

TIP

Make the buttons on the costume by embroidering tiny French knots!

Yarn

100% 4-ply cotton; colours used: **skin** colour, **dark grey**, **white**, **light grey**, **peach**, **sage green**, **brown**, **rose**, small amount of **pink**

Hooks

Size 2mm (US B/1) hook

Other Tools and Materials

Stitch marker

Safety eyes, 2 x 6mm (¼in)

Fibrefill stuffing

A little piece of craft wire, 3cm (1⅕in) to create a small ring for nose piercing

Round-nose pliers

Finished size

15cm (6in) tall

Taurus

20 April–20 May

The 2nd sign of the Zodiac

Tenacious, determined and hard-working, Taureans are calm and reserved beings, not too fond of change or of being pushed into hasty decisions. If you do push them, beware of their temper! This earth sign loves nature and spending time in the outdoors, savouring the fresh air and taking care of plants and flowers. Ruled by Venus, the planet of beauty and harmony, Taurus tends to have artistic skills, a beautiful voice, a love for cooking and a strong faith in romance and passion. Of one thing you can be sure: such a stable and empathic person makes a faithful and trustworthy friend to last a lifetime!

Symbol	Depiction	Element	Ruling Planet	Lucky Gemstone

Best Character Trait: Strength

Lucky Colour: Green

Notable Taurus People: Pyotr Ilyich Tchaikovsky, Florence Nightingale, Stevie Wonder & Queen Elizabeth II

Makes Good Friends With: Virgo, Capricorn & Pisces

Leg 1

Round 1: Using **dark grey** for the boots, 6 sc in a magic ring. (6 sts)
Round 2: 2 sc in each st. (12 sts)
Round 3: 1 sc BLO in each st.
Rounds 4 to 7: 1 sc in each st.
Round 8: Change to **skin** colour, 1 sc BLO in each st.
Rounds 9 and 10: 1 sc in each st.
Fasten off invisibly. Set aside.

Leg 2

Work as for Leg 1 to the end of round 10.
Round 11: Change to **white**, 1 sc BLO in each st.
Do not fasten off yarn. We will continue with the body.

Body

Still with leg 2 on your hook, ch 3 and join to leg 1 with a sc in the back loop of any stitch of leg 1 (*see Techniques: Joining Legs – Option 1*). Work a further 11 sc through the back loops along leg 1.
Round 12: Place a stitch marker on the first stitch for beg of new round, 1 sc into each ch of 3-ch-loop, 12 sc all along leg 2, 1 sc into other side of each ch of 3-ch-loop, 12 sc all along leg 1. (30 sts)
Rounds 13 to 16: 1 sc in each st.
Round 17: Change to **Light Grey**, 1 sc in each st.
Round 18: 1 sc BLO in each st.
Round 19: *3 sc, sc2tog; rep from * to end. (24 sts)
Round 20: Change to **skin** colour, 1 sc BLO in each st.

Rounds 21 and 22: 1 sc in each st.
Round 23: Change to **white**, 1 sc BLO in each st.
Round 24: *2 sc, sc2tog; rep from * to end. (18 sts)
Stuff the body firmly at this point.
Rounds 25 and 26: 1 sc in each st.
Round 27: *1 sc, sc2tog; rep from * to end. (12 sts)
Rounds 28 and 29: 1 sc in each st.
Round 30: Change to **skin** colour, 1 sc BLO in each st.
Round 31: 1 sc in each st.
Do not fasten off yarn. We will continue with the head.

Head

Round 32: 2 sc in each st. (24 sts)
Round 33: *1 sc, 2 sc in the next st; rep from * to end. (36 sts)
Stuff the neck area firmly at this point.
Round 34: *5 sc, 2 sc in the next st; rep from * to end. (42 sts)
Rounds 35 and 36: 1 sc in each st.
Round 37: sc in each st until you are above the middle of the legs at the front of the body, 1 bobble st for the nose (*see Stitches: Bobble st*), sc in each st to end.
Rounds 38 to 47: 1 sc in each st.
Round 48: *5 sc, sc2tog; rep from * to end. (36 sts)
Place safety eyes one round above the nose, with 8 sts between them, embroider cheeks with **pink** yarn.
Round 49: *4 sc, sc2tog; rep from * to end. (30 sts)
Round 50: *3 sc, sc2tog; rep from * to end. (24 sts)

Start stuffing the head at this point.
Round 51: *2 sc, sc2tog; rep from * to end. (18 sts)
Round 52: *1 sc, sc2tog; rep from * to end. (12 sts)
Stuff firmly.
Round 53: (sc2tog) 6 times. (6 sts)
Fasten off and weave in ends.

Pleated Skirt

Turn the doll's body upside down and join the **light grey** yarn with a slip knot in one of the front loops of round 18 at the back of the body.
Ch 8, 1 sc in the second ch from hook, 1 sc in each ch to end (7 sc), *1 slst in next front loop of round 18, turn, 1 sc BLO in each st of skirt, ch 1, turn, 1 sc BLO in each st to end (7 sc); rep from * until each st from round 18 has been worked.
Fasten off, leaving a long tail to sew both ends of the skirt.
Thread your tapestry needle with the remaining yarn tail and sew both ends of the skirt together.

Arms (Make Two)

Round 1: Using **skin** colour, ch 2, 4 sc in the second ch from hook. (4 sts)

Round 2: 2 sc in each st. (8 sts)

Rounds 3 to 16: 1 sc in each st.

Round 17: Press the opening with your fingers, aligning 4 sts side by side and sc both sides together by working 1 sc into each pair of sts (*see Techniques: Closing the Arms*).

Fasten off, leaving a long tail to sew to the body.

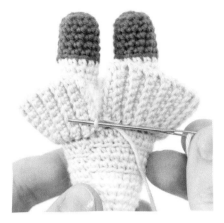

Vest

The vest is worked in rows using a 2mm hook and **dark grey**.

Row 1: Ch 17, 1 sc in the second ch from hook, 1 sc in each ch to end, ch 1, turn. (16 sc).

Row 2: 2 sc, ch 6, skip the following 4 sts (to create first armhole), 4 sc, ch 6, skip the following 4 sts (to create second armhole), 2 sc, ch 1, turn.

Row 3: 2 sc, 6 sc in the first 6-ch-loop, 4 sc, 6 sc in the second 6-ch-loop, 2 sc, ch 1, turn. (20 sts).

Rows 4 to 9: 1 sc in each st, ch 1, turn.

Row 10: 1 sc in each st, ch 1, rotate the work 90 degrees clockwise and work 9 sc along the side of the vest, working in the spaces between rows. When you reach the top edge, crochet 16 sc in the remaining loops of the foundation chain, ch 1, rotate the piece 90 degrees clockwise again and work 10 sc along the other side of the vest, working in the spaces between rows. Fasten off and weave in ends.

Hair

Round 1: Using **peach** for the hair, 6 sc in a magic ring. (6 sts)

Round 2: 2 sc in each st. (12 sts)

Round 3: *1 sc, 2 sc in the next st; rep from * to end. (18 sts)

Round 4: *2 sc, 2 sc in the next st; rep from * to end. (24 sts)

Round 5: *3 sc, 2 sc in the next st; rep from * to end. (30 sts)

Round 6: *4 sc, 2 sc in the next st; rep from * to end. (36 sts)

Round 7: *5 sc, 2 sc in the next st; rep from * to end. (42 sts)

Round 8: *13 sc, 2 sc in the next st; rep from * to end. (45 sts)

Rounds 9 to 16: 1 sc in each st.

Round 17: 1 slst, 1 sc, 1 hdc, 8 dc, 1 hdc, 1 sc, 2 slst, * ch 4, 1 sc in second ch from hook, 1 sc in each st along ch (3 sts), 2 slst; rep from * once more, 1 sc, 1 hdc, 4 dc, 1 hdc, 1 sc, 1 slst. Leave the rest of the stitches unworked.

Fasten off, leaving a long tail to sew to the head. Sew the hair to the head now, and when doing so, secure the two short hairlocks to her forehead.

Braids (Make Two)

Cut 18 strands, each 20cm long, using your **peach** yarn. Choose three stitches on one side of your doll's head, on the edge of the hair piece. With your yarn needle, pass three strands through each stitch, folding them in half. Take the strands and braid them. Tie them with a bit of the **light grey** yarn used for her skirt. Trim the ends to make the braid tidier. Repeat this with the second braid on the other side.

Beanie

Round 1: Using **light grey** for the beanie, 6 sc in a magic ring. (6 sts)
Round 2: 1 sc in each st.
Round 3: 2 sc in each st. (12 sts)
Round 4: 1 sc in each st.
Round 5: *1 sc, 2 sc in the next st; rep from * to end. (18 sts)
Round 6: 1 sc in each st.
Round 7: *2 sc, 2 sc in the next st; rep from * to end. (24 sts)
Round 8: 1 sc in each st.
Round 9: *3 sc, 2 sc in the next st; rep from * to end. (30 sts)
Round 10: 1 sc in each st.
Round 11: *4 sc, 2 sc in the next st; rep from * to end. (36 sts)
Round 12: 1 sc in each st.
Round 13: *5 sc, 2 sc in the next st; rep from * to end. (42 sts)
Round 14: 1 sc in each st.
Round 15: *6 sc, 2 sc in the next st; rep from * to end. (48 sts)
Round 16: *23 sc, 2 sc in the next st; rep from * to end. (50 sts)
Rounds 17 to 21: 1 sc in each st.
Round 22: Ch 2, 1 dc BLO in each st.
Fasten off and weave in ends.

Ribbon

Round 1: Using **dark grey**, ch 50.
Fasten off, leaving a long tail to sew to the tip of the beanie.

Bull Horns (Make Two)

Round 1: Using **dark grey**, ch 2, 4 sc in the second ch from hook. (4 sts)
Round 2: *1 sc, 2 sc in the next st; rep from * to end. (6 sts)
Round 3: 1 sc in each st.
Round 4: *2 sc, 2 sc in the next st; rep from * to end. (8 sts)
Round 5: 1 sc in each st.
Round 6: 2 sc in the next 4 sts, 1 sc in the remaining 4 sts. (12 sts)
Rounds 7 and 8: 1 sc in each st.
Fasten off, leaving a long tail to sew to the beanie.

Plant

The Soil

Round 1: Using **brown** for the soil, 6 sc in a magic ring. (6 sts)

Round 2: 2 sc in each st. (12 sts)

Round 3: *1 sc, 2 sc in the next st; rep from * to end. (18 sts)

Round 4: *2 sc, 2 sc in the next st; rep from * to end. (24 sts)

Fasten off and weave in ends.

The Pot

Round 1: Using **rose** for the pot, 6 sc in a magic ring. (6 sts)

Round 2: 2 sc in each st. (12 sts)

Round 3: *1 sc, 2 sc in the next st; rep from * to end. (18 sts)

Round 4: 1 sc BLO in each st.

Rounds 5 and 6: 1 sc in each st.

Round 7: *8 sc, 2 sc in the next st; rep from * once more. (20 sts)

Round 8: 1 sc in each st.

Round 9: *9 sc, 2 sc in the next st; rep from * once more. (22 sts)

Round 10: 1 sc in each st.

Round 11: *10 sc, 2 sc in the next st; rep from * once more. (24 sts)

Stuff firmly. Take the soil piece and place it over the opening of the pot.

Round 12: 1 sc joining one st of the opening of the pot with one st of the soil, rep from * to the end. Before fully closing the opening, check if you need to add more stuffing.

Fasten off and weave in ends.

Edge of the Pot

Turn the pot upside down and join the **rose** yarn in one of the front loops of the stitches of the last round of the pot.

Round 1: *11 sc FLO, 2 sc FLO in the next st; rep from * once more. (26 sts)

Round 2: 1 sc in each st.

Fasten off and weave in ends.

Leaves (Make Three)

Round 1: Using **sage green** ch 11, 1 slst in the second ch from hook, 2 sc, 3 hdc, 2 sc, 1 slst, 3 slst in the last st of the chain (this will allow you to turn and work on the other side of the chain), 1 slst, 2 sc, 3 hdc, 2 sc, 1 slst.

Close with a slst in the first stitch. Fasten off, leaving a long tail to sew to the pot.

Assembly

Sew the arms to the sides of the body (*see Techniques: Sewing the Arms*).

Stuff the bull's horns a little and sew them to the beanie, curving the tips.

Sew the ribbon to the tip of the beanie forming three loops.

Slip the vest up the arms.

Embroider a little heart on one of the arms as a tattoo using **dark grey** yarn.

Place the little wire ring on the nose as a piercing.

Sew the leaves to the pot.

Weave in all ends inside the doll and the pot.

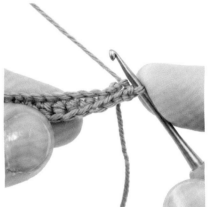

TIP

If you are planning on giving this doll to a small child, you should not add the piercing onto the nose.

Gemini

21 May-20 June

The 3rd sign of the Zodiac

Hello to the most sociable and playful sign of all! The twins are here and they don't like to be bored. True citizens of the world, they love to travel and see new places. So get ready to come up with lots of activities and ideas to stimulate your very curious Gemini friends. And don't worry, you'll have fun too, since they are funny, quick-witted and love making others laugh! Ruled by loquacious Mercury, Geminis are the most gifted communicators in the Zodiac and know very well how to pull a prank or two with their wit and humour. They can easily become the heart and soul of any gathering!

Symbol	Depiction	Element	Ruling Planet	Lucky Gemstone

Best Character Trait: Adaptability
Lucky Colour: Yellow
Notable Gemini People: John F. Kennedy, Marilyn Monroe, Paul McCartney & Judy Garland
Makes Good Friends With: Libra, Aquarius & Aries

Yarn

100% 4-ply cotton; colours used: **skin** colour, **white**, **pale yellow**, **light blue**, **powder rose**, **curry**, small amount of **pink**

Hooks

Size 2mm (US B/1) hook

Other Tools and Materials

Stitch marker

Safety eyes, 4 x 6mm (¼in)

Fibrefill stuffing

Finished size

15cm (6in) tall

TIP

The collar should be in line with the nose, so the slst on round 2 should sit right under it. If this is not so, unravel the round and add one or two sc when you begin!

Leg 1

Round 1: Using **skin** colour, 6 sc in a magic ring. (6 sts)
Round 2: 2 sc in each st. (12 sts)
Round 3: 1 sc BLO in each st.
Rounds 4 to 10: 1 sc in each st.
Fasten off invisibly. Set aside.

Leg 2

Work as for Leg 1 to the end of round 10.
Round 11: Change to **white**, 1 sc BLO in each st.
Do not fasten off yarn. We will continue with the body.

Body

Still with leg 2 on your hook, ch 3 and join to leg 1 with a sc in the back loop of any stitch of leg 1 (*see Techniques: Joining Legs – Option 1*). Work further 11 sc through the back loops along leg 1.
Round 12: Place a stitch marker on the first stitch for beg of new round, 1 sc into each ch of 3-ch-loop, 12 sc all along leg 2, 1 sc into other side of each ch of 3-ch-loop, 12 sc all along leg 1. (30 sts)
Rounds 13 to 17: 1 sc in each st.
Round 18: Change to **pale yellow** for Twin 1 or **light blue** for Twin 2, 1 sc BLO in each st.
Round 19: *3 sc, sc2tog; rep from * to end. (24 sts)
Rounds 20 to 22: 1 sc in each st.
Round 23: *2 sc, sc2tog; rep from * to end. (18 sts)
Stuff the body firmly at this point.
Rounds 24 to 26: 1 sc in each st.
Round 27: *1 sc, sc2tog; rep from * to end. (12 sts)
Rounds 28 and 29: 1 sc in each st.
Round 30: Change to **skin** colour, 1 sc BLO in each st.
Round 31: 1 sc in each st.
Do not fasten off yarn. We will continue with the head.

Head

Round 32: 2 sc in each st. (24 sts)
Round 33: *1 sc, 2 sc in the next st; rep from * to end. (36 sts)
Stuff the neck area firmly at this point.
Round 34: *5 sc, 2 sc in the next st; rep from * to end. (42 sts)
Rounds 35 and 36: 1 sc in each st.
Round 37: sc in each st until you are above the middle of the legs at the front of the body, 1 bobble st for the nose (*see Stitches: Bobble st*), sc in each st to end.

We will now start crocheting the collar of the shirt, as it will be easier to do so without the head in place. Place a stitch marker in the loop on your hook to secure it and cut the yarn.

Collar

Turn the body upside down and join **pale yellow** for Twin 1 or **light blue** for Twin 2 in one of the front loops of round 30, at the back of the neck.
Round 1: 1 sc FLO in each st of round 30. (12 sts)
Round 2: 4 sc, (1 hdc, 1 dc) all in the next st, (3 dc) all in the next st, 1 slst, (1 slst, ch 2, 2 dc) all in the next st, (1 dc, 1 hdc) all in the next st, 3 sc. (16 sts)
Fasten off and weave in ends.

We will now continue with the head. Rejoin yarn to where you stopped working the head previously
Rounds 38 to 47: Using **skin** colour, 1 sc in each st.
Round 48: *5 sc, sc2tog; rep from * to end. (36 sts)
Place safety eyes one round above the nose, with 8 sts between them, embroider cheeks with **pink** yarn.
Round 49: *4 sc, sc2tog; rep from * to end. (30 sts)
Round 50: *3 sc, sc2tog; rep from * to end. (24 sts)
Start stuffing the head at this point.
Round 51: *2 sc, sc2tog; rep from * to end. (18 sts)
Round 52: *1 sc, sc2tog; rep from * to end. (12 sts)
Stuff firmly.
Round 53: (sc2tog) 6 times. (6 sts)
Fasten off and weave in ends.

Arms (Make Two)

Round 1: Using **skin** colour, ch 2, 4 sc in the second ch from hook. (4 sts)

Round 2: 2 sc in each st. (8 sts)

Rounds 3 to 12: 1 sc in each st.

Round 13: Change to **pale yellow** for Twin 1 or **light blue** for Twin 2, 1 sc BLO in each st.

Rounds 14 to 16: 1 sc in each st.

Round 17: Press the opening with your fingers, aligning 4 sts side by side and sc both sides together by working 1 sc into each pair of sts (*see Techniques: Closing the Arms*).

Fasten off, leaving a long tail to sew to the body.

Ear (Make One)

Round 1: Using **skin** colour, 6 sc in a magic ring. (6 sts)

Close the ring with a sl st into the first sc and fasten off, leaving a long tail to sew to the head.

Jumper Dress

Round 1: Using **light blue** for Twin 1 or **pale yellow** for Twin 2, ch 30, 1 sc in the 1st chain (that's the 30th chain from hook) to form a ring (be sure not to twist the chain). 1 sc in each ch to end. (30 sts)

Round 2: 1 sc in each st.

Round 3: 1 sc BLO in each st.

Round 4: *4 sc, 2 sc in the next st; rep from * to end. (36 sts)

Round 5: 1 sc in each st.

Round 6: *5 sc, 2 sc in the next st; rep from * to end. (42 sts)

Rounds 7 to 9: 1 sc in each st.

Fasten off and weave in ends.

Front Bib

Using **light blue** for Twin 1 or **pale yellow** for Twin 2, join the yarn on the top edge of the skirt with a slip knot in the 12th stitch from the right edge.

Row 1: 1 sc in the next 6 sts, ch 1, turn. (6 sts)

Rows 2 to 4: 1 sc in each st, ch 1, turn.

Row 5: 1 sc in each st, ch 1, rotate the work 90 degrees clockwise and work 4 sc along the side of the bib, working in the spaces between rows.

Fasten off and weave in ends.

Strap

Using **light blue** for Twin 1 or **pale yellow** for Twin 2, join the yarn with a slip knot in the corner of the join between the skirt and the front bib on the right hand edge of the bib.

Work 5 sc along the side of the bib, working in the spaces between rows. When you reach the top edge, ch 20 to create the strap.

Fasten off, leaving a long tail to sew.

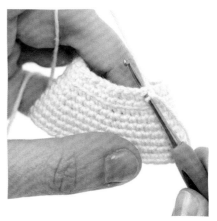

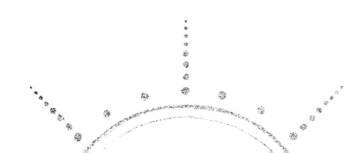

Hair 1 (Twin 1 - with pigtail to the right)

Round 1: Using **powder rose** for the hair, 6 sc in a magic ring. (6 sts)

Round 2: 2 sc in each st. (12 sts)

Round 3: *1 sc, 2 sc in the next st; rep from * to end. (18 sts)

Round 4: *2 sc, 2 sc in the next st; rep from * to end. (24 sts)

Round 5: *3 sc, 2 sc in the next st; rep from * to end. (30 sts)

Round 6: *4 sc, 2 sc in the next st; rep from * to end. (36 sts)

Round 7: *5 sc, 2 sc in the next st; rep from * to end. (42 sts)

Round 8: *13 sc, 2 sc in the next st; rep from * to end. (45 sts)

Rounds 9 to 16: 1 sc in each st.

Round 17: *1 slst, ch 16, 1 sc in second ch from hook, 1 sc in each st along ch (15 sts); rep from * once more, 16 sc, ch 31, 1 sc in second ch from hook, 1 sc in each st along ch (30 sts), 1 slst, 1 sc, 1 hdc, 5 dc, 1 hdc, 1 sc, 1 slst. Leave the rest of the stitches unworked.

Fasten off, leaving a long tail to sew to the head.

Hair 2 (Twin 2 - with pigtail to the left)

Work as for hair 1 to the end of round 6.

Round 17: 1 slst, 1 sc, 1 hdc, 5 dc, 1 hdc, 1 sc, 1 slst, ch 31, 1 sc in second ch from hook, 1 sc in each st along ch (30 sts), 16 sc, *1 slst, ch 16, 1 sc in second ch from hook, 1 sc in each st along ch (15 sts), rep from * once more, 1 slst. Leave the rest of the stitches unworked.

Fasten off, leaving a long tail to sew to the head.

Straw Hat

Round 1: Using **curry** for the hat, 6 sc in a magic ring. (6 sts)
Round 2: 2 sc in each st. (12 sts)
Round 3: *1 sc, 2 sc in the next st; rep from * to end. (18 sts)
Round 4: *2 sc, 2 sc in the next st; rep from * to end. (24 sts)
Round 5: *3 sc, 2 sc in the next st; rep from * to end. (30 sts)
Round 6: *4 sc, 2 sc in the next st; rep from * to end. (36 sts)
Round 7: *5 sc, 2 sc in the next st; rep from * to end. (42 sts)
Rounds 8 to 10: 1 sc in each st.
Round 11: *6 sc, 2 sc in the next st; rep from * to end. (48 sts)
Rounds 12 to 13: 1 sc in each st.
Round 14: *23 sc, 2 sc in the next st; rep from * to end. (50 sts)
Rounds 15 to 16: 1 sc in each st.
Round 17: *1 sc BLO, 2 sc BLO in the next st; rep from * to end. (75 sts)
Round 18: 1 sc in each st.
Round 19: *4 sc, 2 sc in the next st; rep from * to end. (90 sts)
Round 20: 1 sc in each st.
Round 21: 1 slst in each st.
Fasten off and weave in ends.

Assembly

Sew the hair to the head (*see Techniques: Sewing the Hair*), with the long lock on her forehead, slightly to one side. Part the hairlock towards the pigtail and tie them together with a bit of yarn in the same colour as the jumper for the doll you are making.
Sew the ear to the other side of the head, the one with no pigtail.
Sew the arms to the sides of the body (*see Techniques: Sewing the Arms*). You might need to lift the collar slightly.
Slip up the legs through the dress and surround the neck from the back with the strap.
Sew the end of the strap to the other side of the front bib.
Place the straw hat on the head.
Weave in all ends inside the doll.

TIP

There's no need to actually sew the long hair lock to the head. Just tie it to the other locks to create the pigtail.

Cancer

21 June-21 July
The 4th sign of the Zodiac

Do not be fooled by the hard outer shell protecting the crab, inside you will find a sensitive, clever, and vulnerable soul with strong emotions. Like the tides, Cancerians are ruled by the Moon, which means that energy and emotions go up and down for them. But this also makes them deeply empathic, loyal, and caring, almost maternal. Although shy at first, they can create strong bonds and are very protective of their friends. Cancerians are usually quite tenacious too, so if something is caught on their pincers, they won't give it up easily!

| Symbol | Depiction | Element | Ruling Planet | Lucky Gemstone |

Best Character Trait: Compassion
Lucky Colour: Silver
Notable Cancer People: Alan Turing, Princess Diana, Nelson Mandela, & Malala Yousafzai
Makes Good Friends With: Taurus, Cancer & Aquarius

Yarn

100% 4-ply cotton; colours used: **skin** colour, **dark red**, **wine red**, small amount of **pink**

Hooks

Size 2mm (US B/1) hook

Other Tools and Materials

Stitch marker

Safety eyes, 2 x 6mm (¼in)

Fibrefill stuffing

Finished size

15cm (6in) tall

Leg 1

Round 1: Using **skin** colour, 6 sc in a magic ring. (6 sts)
Round 2: 2 sc in each st. (12 sts)
Round 3: 1 sc BLO in each st.
Rounds 4 to 7: 1 sc in each st.
Round 8: Change to **wine red**, 1 sc BLO in each st
Rounds 9 to 11: 1 sc in each st.
Fasten off invisibly. Set aside.

Leg 2

Work as for Leg 1 but do not fasten off yarn. We will continue with the body.

Body

Round 12: Still with leg 2 on your hook, ch 3 and join to leg 1 with a sc in any stitch of leg 1 (see Techniques: Joining Legs – Option 2), place a stitch marker here for new beg of round, work a further 11 sc along leg 1, 1 sc into each ch of 3-ch-loop, 12 sc all along leg 2, 1 sc into other side of each ch of 3-ch-loop. (30 sts)
Rounds 13 to 18: 1 sc in each st.
Round 19: *3 sc, sc2tog; rep from * to end. (24 sts)
Round 20: Change to **skin** colour, 1 sc BLO in each st.
Rounds 21 and 22: 1 sc in each st.
Round 23: *2 sc, sc2tog; rep from * to end. (18 sts)
Stuff the body firmly at this point.

Rounds 24 to 27: 1 sc in each st.
Round 28: *1 sc, sc2tog; rep from * to end. (12 sts)
Round 29: Change to **dark red**, 1 sc in each st.
Round 30: Change to **wine red**, 1 sc BLO in each st.
Round 31: 1 sc in each st.
Round 32: Change to **skin** colour, 1 sc BLO in each st.
Do not fasten off yarn. We will continue with the head.

Head

Round 33: 2 sc in each st. (24 sts)
Round 34: *1 sc, 2 sc in the next st; rep from * to end. (36 sts)
Stuff the neck area firmly at this point.
Round 35: *5 sc, 2 sc in the next st; rep from * to end. (42 sts)
Rounds 36 and 37: 1 sc in each st.
Round 38: sc in each st until you are above the middle of the legs at the front of the body, 1 bobble st for the nose (see Stitches: Bobble st), sc in each st to end.

We will now start crocheting the dress, it will be easier to do so without the finished head. Place a stitch marker in the loop on your hook to secure it and cut the yarn.

Dress

Turn the body upside down and join **dark red** yarn in one of the front loops of round 30, at the back of the neck.

Round 1: 1 sc FLO in each st of round 30. (12 sts)
Round 2: *1 sc, 2 sc in the next st; rep from * to end. (18 sts)
Round 3: 1 sc in each st.
Round 4: *2 sc, 2 sc in the next st; rep from * to end. (24 sts)
Rounds 5 to 7: 1 sc in each st.
Round 8: *3 sc, 2 sc in the next st; rep from * to end. (30 sts)
Rounds 9 to 12: 1 sc in each st.
Round 13: *4 sc, 2 sc in the next st; rep from * to end. (36 sts)
Rounds 12 to 17: 1 sc in each st.
Round 18: *1 slst, 1 sc, (1 hdc, 1 dc, 1 hdc) all in the next st, 1 sc; rep from * to end, 1 slst in the first st of the round to finish. (55 sts) Fasten off invisibly and weave in ends.

We will now continue with the head. Rejoin the **skin** colour yarn to where you stopped working the head.
Rounds 39 to 48: 1 sc in each st.
Round 49: *5 sc, sc2tog; rep from * to end. (36 sts)
Place safety eyes one round above the nose, with 8 sts between them, embroider cheeks with **pink** yarn.
Round 50: *4 sc, sc2tog; rep from * to end. (30 sts)
Round 51: *3 sc, sc2tog; rep from * to end. (24 sts)
Start stuffing the head at this point.
Round 52: *2 sc, sc2tog; rep from * to end. (18 sts)
Round 53: *1 sc, sc2tog; rep from * to end. (12 sts)
Stuff firmly.
Round 54: (sc2tog) 6 times. (6 sts)
Fasten off and weave in ends.

Arms (Make Two)

Round 1: Using **skin** colour, ch 2, 4 sc in the second ch from hook. (4 sts)
Round 2: 2 sc in each st. (8 sts)
Rounds 3 to 10: 1 sc in each st.
Round 11: Change to **dark red**, 1 sc BLO in each st.
Rounds 12 to 14: 1 sc in each st.
Round 16: Press the opening with your fingers, aligning 4 sts side by side and sc both sides together by working 1 sc into each pair of sts (*see Techniques: Closing the Arms*).
Fasten off, leaving a long tail to sew to the body.

TIP

You can decorate the dress as you please! Think of it as a blank canvas! I embroidered little dashes using wine red yarn.

TIP

The little curls on the sides of the hair piece represent the crab's legs. Arrange them so they curl a bit outwards.

Hair

Round 1: Using **dark red** for the hair, 6 sc in a magic ring. (6 sts)
Round 2: 2 sc in each st. (12 sts)
Round 3: *1 sc, 2 sc in the next st; rep from * to end. (18 sts)
Round 4: *2 sc, 2 sc in the next st; rep from * to end. (24 sts)
Round 5: *3 sc, 2 sc in the next st; rep from * to end. (30 sts)
Round 6: *4 sc, 2 sc in the next st; rep from * to end. (36 sts)
Round 7: *5 sc, 2 sc in the next st; rep from * to end. (42 sts)
Round 8: *13 sc, 2 sc in the next st; rep from * to end. (45 sts)
Rounds 9 to 16: 1 sc in each st.
Round 17: *1 slst, ch 9, 1 sc in the second ch from hook, 1 sc in each st along ch (8 sts), 3 sc; rep from * twice more, 1 slst, 1 sc, 1 hdc, 3 dc, 1 hdc, 1 sc, 1 slst, 1 sc, 1 hdc, 3 dc, 1 hdc, 1 sc, 2 slst, **ch 9, 1 sc in the second ch from hook, 1 sc in each st along ch (8 sts), 3 sc, 1 slst; rep from ** once more, ch 9, 1 sc in the second ch from hook, 1 sc in each st along ch (8 sts), 1 slst. Leave the rest of the stitches in the round unworked.
Fasten off, leaving a long tail to sew to the head.

Crab Pincers (Make Two)

Small Claw

Round 1: Using **dark red**, ch 2, 4 sc in the second ch from hook. (4 sts)
Round 2: *1 sc, 2 sc in the next st; rep from * to end. (6 sts)
Round 3: *2 sc, 2 sc in the next st; rep from * to end. (8 sts)
Round 4: 1 sc in each st.
Fasten off invisibly and weave in ends.

Big Claw

Round 1: Using **dark red**, ch 2, 4 sc in the second ch from hook. (4 sts)
Round 2: *1 sc, 2 sc in the next st; rep from * to end. (6 sts)
Round 3: *2 sc, 2 sc in the next st; rep from * to end. (8 sts)
Rounds 4 to 6: 1 sc in each st.
Do not fasten off yarn. We will join both claws together.
Round 7: Still with the big claw on your hook, ch 1 and join to the small claw with a sc in any stitch of the small claw. Place a stitch marker on this first stitch for new beg of round, work a further 7 sc along the small claw, 1 sc into the ch loop, 8 sc all along the big claw, 1 sc into other side of the ch loop. (18 sts)
Rounds 8 and 9: 1 sc in each st.
Stuff both claws firmly.
Round 10: *1 sc, sc2tog; rep from * to end. (12 sts)
Round 12: *1 sc, sc2tog; rep from * to end. (8 sts)
Rounds 13 to 15: 1 sc in each st.
Fasten off, leaving a long tail to sew to the head.

Bow (Make Two)

Row 1: Using **wine red**, ch 11, 1 sc in the second ch from hook, 1 sc in each ch to end, ch 1, turn. (10 sts).
Rows 2 to 4: 1 sc in each st, ch 1, turn.
Row 5: 1 sc in each st, ch 1, rotate the work 90 degrees clockwise and work 4 sc along the side of the piece, working into the spaces between the rows, when you reach the top edge, 10 sc in the remaining loops of the foundation chain, ch 1, rotate the piece 90 degrees clockwise again, 5 sc along the other side of the piece, working in the spaces between rows.
Fasten off and weave in ends.
Wind several rounds of yarn around the middle of the rectangle to create the bow. Once you have done this, finish with a knot on the back of the bow, leaving a tail to sew it to the base of the pincers.

Assembly

Sew the hair to the head (*see Techniques: Sewing the Hair*).
Sew the claws to the hair.
Sew the bows to the base of each claw.
Sew the arms to the sides of the body (*see Techniques: Sewing the Arms*).
Embroider tiny vertical dashes to the dress using **wine red** yarn.
Weave in all ends inside the doll.

Leo

22 July–22 August
The 5th sign of the Zodiac

Prepare to focus the spotlight because Leo is coming, and she loves to be the centre of attention and admiration! Of course, it's easy for her since she has a great sense of style and can be super glamorous and theatrical. Ruled by the mighty Sun, and natural leaders at heart, Leos light up and energize all those around them with their cheerfulness. They are optimistic, creative, charming and always full of hope. Larger-than-life, a Leo friend can move mountains to generously please those she loves the most!

Yarn

100% 4-ply cotton; colours used: **skin** colour, **white**, **sage green**, **toffee**, **orange**, small amount of **pink**

Hook

Size 2mm (US B/1) hook

Other Tools and Materials

Stitch marker

Safety eyes, 2 x 6mm (¼in)

Fibrefill stuffing

Finished size

15cm (6in) tall

Symbol	Depiction	Element	Ruling Planet	Lucky Gemstone

Best Character Trait: Generosity

Lucky Colour: Orange

Notable Leo People: Alexander Fleming, Amelia Earhart, Barack Obama & J.K. Rowling

Makes Good Friends With: Sagittarius, Aries & Libra

Leg 1

Round 1: Using **skin** colour, 6 sc in a magic ring. (6 sts)
Round 2: 2 sc in each st. (12 sts)
Round 3: 1 sc BLO in each st.
Rounds 4 to 7: 1 sc in each st.
Round 8: Change to **sage green**, 1 sc BLO in each st.
Rounds 9 to 11: 1 sc in each st.
Fasten off invisibly. Set aside.

Leg 2

Work as for Leg 1 but do not fasten off yarn. We will continue with the body.

Body

Round 12: Still with leg 2 on your hook, ch 3 and join to leg 1 with a sc in any stitch of leg 1 (see Techniques: Joining Legs – Option 2). Place a stitch marker on the first stitch for beg of new round, work a further 11 sc along leg 1, 1 sc into each ch of 3-ch-loop, 12 sc all along leg 2, 1 sc into other side of each ch of 3-ch-loop. (30 sts)
Rounds 13 to 18: 1 sc in each st.
Round 19: *3 sc, sc2tog; rep from * to end. (24 sts)
Round 20: Change to **skin** colour, 1 sc BLO in each st.
Rounds 21 and 22: 1 sc in each st.
Round 23: *2 sc, sc2tog; rep from * to end. (18 sts)
Stuff the body firmly at this point.
Round 24: 1 sc in each st.
Round 25: Change to **white**, 1 sc in each st.
Round 26: Change back to **skin** colour, 1 sc BLO in each st.
Round 27: 1 sc in each st.
Round 28: *1 sc, sc2tog; rep from * to end. (12 sts)
Rounds 29 to 32: 1 sc in each st.
Do not fasten off yarn. We will continue with the head.

Head

Round 33: 2 sc in each st. (24 sts)
Round 34: *1 sc, 2 sc in the next st; rep from * to end. (36 sts)
Stuff the neck area firmly at this point.
Round 35: *5 sc, 2 sc in the next st; rep from * to end. (42 sts)
Rounds 36 and 37: 1 sc in each st.
Round 38: sc in each st until you are above the middle of the legs at the front of the body, 1 bobble st for the nose (see Stitches: Bobble st), sc in each st to end.
Rounds 39 to 48: 1 sc in each st.
Round 49: *5 sc, sc2tog; rep from * to end. (36 sts)
Place safety eyes one round above the nose, with 8 sts between them, embroider cheeks with **pink** yarn.
Round 50: *4 sc, sc2tog; rep from * to end. (30 sts)
Round 51: *3 sc, sc2tog; rep from * to end. (24 sts)
Start stuffing the head at this point.
Round 52: *2 sc, sc2tog; rep from * to end. (18 sts)
Round 53: *1 sc, sc2tog; rep from * to end. (12 sts)
Stuff firmly.
Round 54: (sc2tog) 6 times. (6 sts)
Fasten off and weave in ends.

TIP

Leo's hair is supposed to look like a mane and it takes time. Make yourself a cup of tea and sit comfortably!

Arms (Make Two)

Round 1: Using **skin** colour, ch 2, 4 sc in the second ch from hook. (4 sts)
Round 2: 2 sc in each st. (8 sts)
Rounds 3 to 16: 1 sc in each st.
Round 17: Press the opening with your fingers, aligning 4 sts side by side and sc both sides together by working 1 sc into each pair of sts (*see Techniques: Closing the Arms*).
Fasten off, leaving a long tail to sew to the body.

Camisole

Turn the body upside down and join **white** yarn in one of the front loops of round 26, at the back of the body.
Round 1: 1 sc in FLO each st of round 26. (18 sts)
Round 2: *2 sc, 2 sc in the next st; rep from * to end. (24 sts)
Round 3: 1 sc in each st.
Round 4: *3 sc, 2 sc in the next st; rep from * to end. (30 sts)
Rounds 5 to 8: 1 sc in each st.
Round 9: *4 sc, 2 sc in the next st; rep from * to end. (36 sts)
Round 10: 1 sc in each st.
Round 11: *1 slst, 1 sc, (1 hdc, 1 dc, 1 hdc) all in the next st, 1 sc; rep from * to end, 1 slst in the first st of the round to finish. (55 sts)
Fasten off and weave in ends.

Straps of the Camisole (Make Two)

Row 1: Using **white** and leaving a long initial tail, ch 12. Measure it against your doll. Bear in mind that the straps should cross over at the back of your doll. Are they too short? Add some extra chain stitches.
Fasten off, leaving a long tail to sew.

Neck Scarf

The scarf is worked in rows. Use **orange**.
Row 1: Ch 61, 1 sc in the second ch from hook, 1 sc in each ch to end, ch 1, turn. (60 sc).
Row 2: 1 sc BLO in each st, ch 1, turn.
Fasten off and weave in ends. Make two tiny pompoms and sew them to the ends of the scarf (*see Techniques: Pompom*).

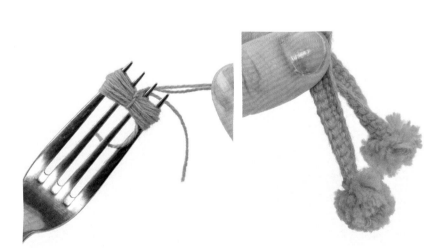

TIP

Make these tiny pompoms using a fork. Alternatively, you could use a small pompom maker and trim to size.

TIP

This hair cap will look much bigger than the head of your doll. Do not worry! It will shrink as you crochet the curls.

Hair

Round 1: Using **toffee**, 6 sc in a magic ring. (6 sts)
Round 2: 2 sc BLO in each st. (12 sts)
Round 3: *1 sc, 2 sc in the next st; rep from * to end. (18 sts)
Round 4: *2 sc BLO, 2 sc BLO in the next st; rep from * to end. (24 sts)
Round 5: *3 sc, 2 sc in the next st; rep from * to end. (30 sts)
Round 6: *4 sc BLO, 2 sc BLO in the next st; rep from * to end. (36 sts)
Round 7: *5 sc, 2 sc in the next st; rep from * to end. (42 sts)
Round 8: *6 sc BLO, 2 sc BLO in the next st; rep from * to end. (48 sts)
Round 9: *7 sc, 2 sc in the next st; rep from * to end. (54 sts)
Round 10: 1 sc BLO in each st.
Round 11: 1 sc in each st.
Round 12: 1 sc BLO in each st.
Round 13: 1 sc in each st.
Round 14: 1 sc BLO in each st.
Round 15: 1 sc in each st.
Round 16: 1 sc BLO in each st.
Fasten off, leaving a long tail to sew to the head.

Curly Hair

If you look at the piece you've just finished, you'll see the spiral of front loops from the magic ring at the beginning, right up to the last round…Now we are going to work the curly hair…

Join the **toffee** yarn in the front loop just above the last stitch you made before closing the last round.

1 sc, ch 11, 1 sc in the second ch from hook, 1 sc in each st along ch (10 sts), 1 slst in the following 3 front loops.

And now let's start stacking up the curls…*ch 11, 1 sc in the second ch from hook, 1 sc in each st along ch (10 sts), 3 slst, rep from * in a spiral to last available front loop at the centre of the spiral at the magic ring.

Fasten off and weave in ends.

The locks will curl naturally as you go…but if they don't, curl them with your fingers as if they were old telephone cables.

Assembly

Sew the hair to the head (*see Techniques: Sewing the Hair*)

Sew the arms to the sides of the body (*see Techniques: Sewing the Arms*).

Sew the straps of the camisole, first on the front and then cross them and sew them to her back.

Wrap the neck with the scarf.

Weave in all ends inside the doll.

Virgo

23 August-22 September

The 6th sign of the Zodiac

Yarn

100% 4-ply cotton; colours used: **skin** colour, **white**, **rose**, **mint**, **dark rose**, small amount of **pink**

Hooks

Size 2mm (US B/1) hook

Other Tools and Materials

Stitch marker

Safety eyes, 2 x 6mm (¼in)

Fibrefill stuffing

Finished size

15cm (6in) tall

Is that a to-do list? Well, practical and neat Virgo will help you sort that out since no one can tackle tasks as efficiently and successfully as her! Doing a job well is very important for busy Virgos, who always aim for perfection. They are all about the details that make things special. Gentle and kind, Virgos love being of service and helping others. Once the chores are done, a good book and a cup of tea can be the best of friends for them!

Symbol	Depiction	Element	Ruling Planet	Lucky Gemstone

Best Character Trait: Organization
Lucky Colour: Blue
Notable Virgo People: Freddy Mercury, Queen Elizabeth I, Mother Theresa & Sean Connery
Makes Good Friends With: Virgo, Taurus & Gemini

Leg 1

Round 1: Using **skin** colour, 6 sc in a magic ring. (6 sts)
Round 2: 2 sc in each st. (12 sts)
Round 3: 1 sc BLO in each st.
Rounds 4 to 10: 1 sc in each st.
Fasten off invisibly. Set aside.

Leg 2

Work as for Leg 1 to the end of round 10.
Round 11: Change to **white**, 1 sc BLO in each st.
Do not fasten off yarn. We will continue with the body.

Body

Still with leg 2 on your hook, ch 3 and join to leg 1 with a sc in the back look of any stitch of leg 1 (*see Techniques: Joining Legs – Option 1*). Work a further 11 sc through the back loops along leg 1.
Round 12: Place a stitch marker on the first stitch for beg of new round, 1 sc into each ch of 3-ch-loop, 12 sc all along leg 2, 1 sc into other side of each ch of 3-ch-loop and 12 sc all along leg 1. (30 sts)
Rounds 13 to 17: 1 sc in each st.
Round 18: Change to **skin** colour, 1 sc BLO in each st.
Round 19: *3 sc, sc2tog; rep from * to end. (24 sts)
Rounds 20 to 22: 1 sc in each st.
Round 23: *2 sc, sc2tog; rep from * to end. (18 sts)
Stuff the body firmly at this point.
Round 24: 1 sc in each st.
Round 25: Change to **rose**, 1 sc in each st.
Round 26: Change back to **skin** colour, 1 sc BLO in each st.
Round 27: *1 sc, sc2tog; rep from * to end. (12 sts)
Rounds 28 to 31: 1 sc in each st.
Do not fasten off yarn. We will continue with the head.

TIP

Virgo is The Maiden of the Zodiac, so choose a pale palette for her. Pastels work beautifully!

Head

Round 32: 2 sc in each st. (24 sts)

Round 33: *1 sc, 2 sc in the next st; rep from * to end. (36 sts)
Stuff the neck area firmly at this point.

Round 34: *5 sc, 2 sc in the next st; rep from * to end. (42 sts)

Rounds 35 and 36: 1 sc in each st.

Round 37: sc in each st until you are above the middle of the legs at the front of the body, 1 bobble st for the nose (*see Stitches: Bobble st*), sc in each st to end.

Rounds 38 to 47: 1 sc in each st.

Round 48: *5 sc, sc2tog; rep from * to end. (36 sts)
Place safety eyes one round above the nose, with 8 sts between them, embroider cheeks with **pink** yarn.

Round 49: *4 sc, sc2tog; rep from * to end. (30 sts)

Round 50: *3 sc, sc2tog; rep from * to end. (24 sts)
Start stuffing the head at this point.

Round 51: *2 sc, sc2tog; rep from * to end. (18 sts)

Round 52: *1 sc, sc2tog; rep from * to end. (12 sts)
Stuff firmly.

Round 53: (sc2tog) 6 times. (6 sts)
Fasten off and weave in ends.

Arms (Make Two)

Round 1: Using **skin** colour, ch 2, 4 sc in the second ch from hook. (4 sts)

Round 2: 2 sc in each st. (8 sts)

Rounds 3 to 16: 1 sc in each st.

Round 17: Press the opening with your fingers, aligning 4 sts side by side and sc both sides together by working 1 sc into each pair of sts (*see Techniques: Closing the Arms*).
Fasten off, leaving a long tail to sew to the body.

TIP

You can interrupt crocheting the head after round 37 and start with the dress if you want to be able to move your hands freely, without the head interfering.

Dress

Turn the body upside down and join **rose** yarn in one of the front loops of round 26, at the back of the body.

Round 1: 1 sc FLO in each st of round 26. (18 sts)

Round 2: *2 sc, 2 sc in the next st; rep from * to end. (24 sts)

Round 3: 1 sc in each st.

Round 4: *3 sc, 2 sc in the next st; rep from * to end. (30 sts)

Rounds 5 to 7: 1 sc in each st.

Round 8: *4 sc, 2 sc in the next st; rep from * to end. (36 sts)

Rounds 9 to 11: 1 sc in each st.

Round 12: *5 sc, 2 sc in the next st; rep from * to end. (42 sts)

Rounds 13 to 18: 1 sc in each st.

Fasten off and weave in ends.

Strap of the Dress

Row 1: Using **rose** and leaving a long initial tail, ch 17

Fasten off, leaving a long tail to sew around the neck.

Hair

Round 1: Using **white**, 6 sc in a magic ring. (6 sts)

Round 2: 2 sc in each st. (12 sts)

Round 3: *1 sc, 2 sc in the next st; rep from * to end. (18 sts)

Round 4: *2 sc, 2 sc in the next st; rep from * to end. (24 sts)

Round 5: *3 sc, 2 sc in the next st; rep from * to end. (30 sts)

Round 6: *4 sc, 2 sc in the next st; rep from * to end. (36 sts)

Round 7: *5 sc, 2 sc in the next st; rep from * to end. (42 sts)

Round 8: *13 sc, 2 sc in the next st; rep from * to end. (45 sts)

Rounds 9 to 16: 1 sc in each st.

Round 17: 1 slst, 1 sc, 1 hdc, 5 dc, 1 hdc, 1 sc, 2 slst, * ch 7, 1 sc in second ch from hook, 1 sc in each st along ch (6 sts), 1 slst, rep from * twice more to create a fringe,1 sc, 1 hdc, 5 dc, 1 hdc, 1 sc, 1 slst, * ch 21, 1 sc in second ch from hook, 1 sc in each st along ch (20 sts), 1 slst; rep from * to last st. (20 hair curls)

Fasten off, leaving a long tail to sew to the head.

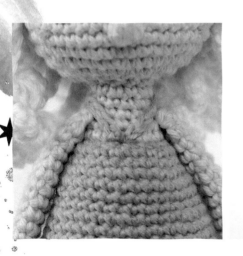

TIP

If you don't secure the fringe with a few stitches, they will curl up and that's lovely too!

Headband

Row 1: Using **rose** and leaving a long initial tail, ch 30
Fasten off, leaving a long tail to sew.

Flowers (Make one in mint and one in dark rose)

Round 1: 5 sc in a magic ring. (5 sts)
Round 2: *1 slst in next st, ch 2, (yarn over, insert hook in same st, pull yarn through st, yarn over, pull yarn through two loops on hook) twice, yarn over, pull yarn through three loops on hook, ch 2, slst in same st, rep from * to end, slst in next st. (5 petals) (*see Techniques: Flowers*).
Fasten off, leaving a long tail to sew to the body.

Assembly

Sew the hair to the head (*see Techniques: Sewing the Hair*), securing the three hairlocks to the forehead.
Sew the arms to the sides of the body (*see Techniques: Sewing the Arms*).
Sew the strap of the dress in the middle of the front of the dress, around the neck and back into the middle of the dress.
Sew the headband to the head using the remaining yarn tails, first from one side, then from the other.
Sew the flowers to one side of the headband.
Weave in all ends inside the doll.

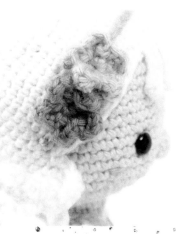

TIP

You can also crochet enough flowers to fully surround Virgo's head.

Yarn

100% 4-ply cotton; colours used: **skin** colour, **white**, **mint**, **pale yellow**, **dark yellow**, small amount of **pink**

Hooks

Size 2mm (US B/1) hook

Other Tools and Materials

Stitch marker

Safety eyes, 2 x 6mm (¼in)

Fibrefill stuffing

Finished size

15cm (6in) tall

Libra

23 September-22 October

The 7th sign of the Zodiac

It's all a question of proportion and equilibrium for balanced Libras: equal amounts of work and play, of reason and emotion. The key is to lead a harmonious life and they sure know how to do so! Well mannered, easy-going and diplomats, they are good at creating peaceful relationships and supporting fair social causes. Ruled by beauty-loving Venus, Libras have a strong inclination towards the Arts, and many are gifted artists, musicians, decorators and even fashionistas.

Symbol	Depiction	Element	Ruling Planet	Lucky Gemstone

Best Character Trait: Fairness

Lucky Colour: Blue

Notable Libra People: Oscar Wilde, Mahatma Gandhi, Julie Andrews & Serena Williams

Makes Good Friends With: Aquarius, Gemini & Leo

Leg 1

Round 1: Using **skin** colour, 6 sc in a magic ring. (6 sts)
Round 2: 2 sc in each st. (12 sts)
Round 3: 1 sc BLO in each st.
Rounds 4 to 10: 1 sc in each st.
Fasten off invisibly. Set aside.

Leg 2

Work as for Leg 1 to the end of round 10.
Round 11: Change to **white**, 1 sc BLO in each st.
Do not fasten off yarn. We will continue with the body.

Body

Still with leg 2 on your hook, ch 3 and join to leg 1 with a sc in the back loop of any stitch of leg 1 (*see Techniques: Joining Legs – Option 1*). Work a further 11 sc through the back loops along leg 1.
Round 12: Place a stitch marker on the first stitch for beg of new round, 1 sc into each ch of 3-ch-loop, 12 sc all along leg 2, 1 sc into other side of each ch of 3-ch-loop, 12 sc all along leg 1. (30 sts)
Rounds 13 to 17: 1 sc in each st.
Round 18: Change to **skin** colour, 1 sc BLO in each st.
Round 19: *3 sc, sc2tog; rep from * to end. (24 sts)
Rounds 20 to 22: 1 sc in each st.
Round 23: *2 sc, sc2tog; rep from * to end. (18 sts)
Stuff the body firmly at this point.
Rounds 24 to 26: 1 sc in each st.
Round 27: *1 sc, sc2tog; rep from * to end. (12 sts)
Rounds 28 to 31: 1 sc in each st.
Do not fasten off yarn. We will continue with the head.

Head

Round 32: 2 sc in each st. (24 sts)
Round 33: *1 sc, 2 sc in the next st; rep from * to end. (36 sts)
Stuff the neck area firmly at this point.
Round 34: *5 sc, 2 sc in the next st; rep from * to end. (42 sts)
Rounds 35 and 36: 1 sc in each st.
Round 37: sc in each st until you are above the middle of the legs at the front of the body, 1 bobble st for the nose (*see Stitches: Bobble st*), sc in each st to end.
Rounds 38 to 47: 1 sc in each st.
Round 48: *5 sc, sc2tog; rep from * to end. (36 sts)
Place safety eyes one round above the nose, with 8 sts between them, embroider cheeks with **pink** yarn.
Round 49: *4 sc, sc2tog; rep from * to end. (30 sts)
Round 50: *3 sc, sc2tog; rep from * to end. (24 sts)
Start stuffing the head at this point.
Round 51: *2 sc, sc2tog; rep from * to end. (18 sts)
Round 52: *1 sc, sc2tog; rep from * to end. (12 sts)
Stuff firmly.
Round 53: (sc2tog) 6 times. (6 sts)
Fasten off and weave in ends.

Arms (Make Two)

Round 1: Using **skin** colour, ch 2, 4 sc in the second ch from hook. (4 sts)

Round 2: 2 sc in each st. (8 sts)

Rounds 3 to 16: 1 sc in each st.

Round 17: Press the opening with your fingers, aligning 4 sts side by side and sc both sides together by working 1 sc into each pair of sts (*see Techniques: Closing the Arms*).

Fasten off, leaving a long tail to sew to the body.

Dress

Bodice of the Dress

Row 1: Using **white**, leave a long initial tail and ch 25, 1 sc in the second ch from hook, 1 sc in each ch to end, ch 1, turn. (24 sts).

Row 2: 3 sc, ch 6, skip the following 6 sts (to create first armhole), 6 sc, ch 6, skip the following 6 sts (to create second armhole), 3 sc, ch 1, turn.

Row 3: 3 sc, 6 sc in the first 6-ch-loop, 6 sc, 6 sc in the second 6-ch-loop, 3 sc, ch 1, turn. (24 sts)

Row 4: 1 sc in each st.

Do not fasten off yarn. We will continue with the pleated skirt.

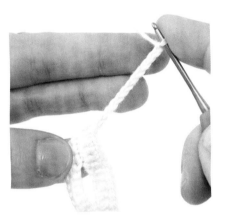

Pleated Skirt

Row 1: Ch 13, 1 sc in the second ch from hook, 1 sc in each ch to end (12 sc), 1 slst in the next st of the bodice.

Row 2: Turn, 1 sc BLO in each st of the previous row of the pleat. (12 sc)

Row 3: Ch 1, turn, 1 sc BLO in each st to the last row of the bodice, 1 slst in the next stitch along the bodice.

Rows 4 to 24: Repeat rows 2 and 3 until you have worked all the stitches of the last row of the bodice.

Fasten off, leaving a long tail to sew.

Hair

Round 1: Using **mint**, 6 sc in a magic ring. (6 sts)
Round 2: 2 sc in each st. (12 sts)
Round 3: *1 sc, 2 sc in the next st; rep from * to end. (18 sts)
Round 4: *2 sc, 2 sc in the next st; rep from * to end. (24 sts)
Round 5: *3 sc, 2 sc in the next st; rep from * to end. (30 sts)
Round 6: *4 sc, 2 sc in the next st; rep from * to end. (36 sts)
Round 7: *5 sc, 2 sc in the next st; rep from * to end. (42 sts)
Round 8: *13 sc, 2 sc in the next st; rep from * to end. (45 sts)
Rounds 9 to 16: 1 sc in each st.
Round 17: *1 slst, 1 sc, (1 hdc, 1 dc, 1 hdc) all in the next st, 1 sc, 1 slst; rep from * to end. (63 sts)
Fasten off, leaving a long tail to sew to the head.

Hair Buns (Make Two)

Round 1: Using **mint**, 5 sc in a magic ring. (5 sts)
Round 2: 2 sc in each st. (10 sts)
Round 3: *1 sc, 2 sc in the next st; rep from * to end. (15 sts)
Round 4: *2 sc, 2 sc in the next st; rep from * to end. (20 sts)
Rounds 5 to 7: 1 sc in each st.
Round 8: *2 sc, sc2tog; rep from * to end. (15 sts)
Fasten off, leaving a long tail to sew to the hair.

Scales (Make Two)

Inner Layer

Round 1: Using **pale yellow**, 6 sc in a magic ring. (6 sts)
Round 2: 2 sc in each st. (12 sts)
Round 3: *1 sc, 2 sc in the next st; rep from * to end. (18 sts)
Round 4: *2 sc, 2 sc in the next st; rep from * to end. (24 sts)
Round 5: 1 sc in each st.
Fasten off and weave in ends.
Turn the inner layer inside out. Set aside.

TIP

Don't forget to turn the inner layer of the scale inside-out!

Outer Layer

Round 1: Using **dark yellow**, 6 sc in a magic ring. (6 sts)
Round 2: 2 sc in each st. (12 sts)
Round 3: *1 sc, 2 sc in the next st, rep from * to end. (18 sts)
Round 4: *2 sc, 2 sc in the next st, rep from * to end. (24 sts)
Rounds 5 to 6: 1 sc in each st.
Take the inner layer and place it inside the outer layer.
Round 7: 1 sc joining one st of the inner layer with one st of the outer layer, 1 slst to finish.
Fasten off, leaving a long tail to pass through the arms.

Assembly

Sew the hair to the head (*see Techniques: Sewing the Hair*).
Stuff and sew the hair-buns to the sides of the hair. Wrap them with a bit of pink yarn.
Sew the arms to the sides of the body (*see Techniques: Sewing the Arms*).
Put the dress on your doll and using a tapestry needle, sew the seam at the back.
Use the long tail on the pleated skirt to sew together the skirt and use the tail at the beginning of row 1 of the bodice of the dress to sew together the bodice.
Pass the long tail remaining on each scale through each arm and sew it onto the other side of the scale as illustrated. Make sure to achieve the same height on both scales.
Weave in all ends inside the doll.

TIP

Libra is all about equilibrium and balance. Make sure the hair-buns look symmetrical.

Yarn

100% 4ply-cotton; colours used: **skin** colour, **white**, **black**, **red**, small amount of **pink**

Hooks

Size 2mm (US B/1) hook

Other Tools and Materials

Stitch marker

Safety eyes, 2 x 6mm (¼in)

Fibrefill stuffing

8cm (3⅛in)of coated wire

Round-nose pliers

Finished size

15cm (6in) tall

Scorpio

23 October–21 November

The 8ᵗʰ sign of the Zodiac

Passionate and intense… there's more to Scorpios than meets the eye. They possess powerful emotions, which they prefer to keep hidden from others, under their calm and chill façade. But this much is true: they know what they want and what they need to do to achieve their goals - so you'd better not confront them! Just like real scorpions, Scorpios too can withdraw into themselves to survive the most extreme conditions. However, once you get to know them well, Scorpios like having friends from all walks of life, and they can be truly affectionate and loyal.

Symbol   Depiction   Element   Ruling Planet   Lucky Gemstone

Best Character Trait: Willpower

Lucky Colour: Burgundy

Notable Scorpio People: Pablo Picasso, Hedy Lamarr, Hillary Clinton & Bill Gates

Makes Good Friends With: Cancer, Pisces & Virgo

Leg 1

Round 1: Using **skin** colour, 6 sc in a magic ring. (6 sts)

Round 2: 2 sc in each st. (12 sts)

Round 3: 1 sc BLO in each st

Rounds 4 to 10: 1 sc in each st.
Fasten off invisibly. Set aside.

Leg 2

Work as for Leg 1 to the end of round 10.

Round 11: Change to **white**, 1 sc BLO in each st.
Do not fasten off yarn. We will continue with the body.

Body

Still with leg 2 on your hook, ch 3 and join to leg 1 with a sc in the back loop of any stitch of leg 1 (*see Techniques: Joining Legs – Option 1*). Work a further 11 sc through the back loops along leg 1.

Round 12: Place a stitch marker on the first stitch for beg of new round, 1 sc into each ch of 3-ch-loop, 12 sc all along leg 2, 1 sc into other side of each ch of 3-ch-loop, 12 sc all along leg 1. (30 sts)

Rounds 13 to 16: 1 sc in each st.

Round 17: Change to **black**, 1 sc in each st.

Round 18: Change back to **white**, 1 sc BLO in each st.

Round 19: *3 sc, sc2tog; rep from * to end. (24 sts)

Round 20: Change to **black**, 1 sc in each st.

Round 21: 1 sc in each st.

Round 22: Change to **white**, 1 sc in each st.

Round 23: *2 sc, sc2tog; rep from * to end. (18 sts)
Stuff the body firmly at this point.

Round 24: Change to **black**, 1 sc in each st.

Round 25: 1 sc in each st.

Round 26: Change to **white**, 1 sc in each st.

Round 27: *1 sc, sc2tog; rep from * to end. (12 sts)

Round 28: Change to **black**, 1 sc in each st.

Round 29: 1 sc in each st.

Round 30: Change to **white**, 1 sc in each st.

Round 31: 1 sc in each st.
Do not fasten off yarn. We will continue with the head.

Head

Round 32: Change to **skin** colour, 1 sc BLO in each st.

Round 33: 2 sc in each st. (24 sts)

Round 34: *1 sc, 2 sc in the next st; rep from * to end. (36 sts)
Stuff the neck area firmly at this point.

Round 35: *5 sc, 2 sc in the next st; rep from * to end. (42 sts)

Rounds 36 and 37: 1 sc in each st.

Round 38: sc in each st until you are above the middle of the legs at the front of the body, 1 bobble st for the nose (*see Stitches: Bobble st*), sc in each st to end.

Rounds 39 to 47: 1 sc in each st.

Round 48: *5 sc, sc2tog; rep from * to end. (36 sts)
Place safety eyes one round above the nose, with 8 sts between them, embroider cheeks with **pink** yarn.

Round 49: *4 sc, sc2tog; rep from * to end. (30 sts)

Round 50: *3 sc, sc2tog; rep from * to end. (24 sts)
Start stuffing the head at this point.

Round 51: *2 sc, sc2tog; rep from * to end. (18 sts)

Round 52: *1 sc, sc2tog; rep from * to end. (12 sts)
Stuff firmly.

Round 53: (sc2tog) 6 times. (6 sts)
Fasten off and weave in ends.

Arms (Make Two)

Round 1: Using **skin** colour, ch 2, 4 sc in the second ch from hook. (4 sts)

Round 2: 2 sc in each st. (8 sts)

Rounds 3 to 16: 1 sc in each st.

Round 17: Press the opening with your fingers, aligning 4 sts side by side and sc both sides together by working 1 sc into each pair of sts (*see Techniques: Closing the Arms*).

Fasten off, leaving a long tail to sew to the body.

Skirt

Turn the body upside down and join **black** yarn in one of the front loops of round 18, at the back of the body.

Round 1: 1 sc FLO in each st of round 18. (30 sts)

Round 2: *4 sc, 2 sc in the next st; rep from * to end. (36 sts)

Round 3: *5 sc, 2 sc in the next st; rep from * to end. (42 sts)

Round 4: 1 sc in each st.

Round 5: 2 sc in each st. (84 sts)

Round 6: *1 sc, 2 sc in the next st; rep from * to end. (126 sts)

Rounds 7 and 8: 1 sc in each st.

Fasten off and weave in ends.

Hair

Round 1: Using **red**, 6 sc in a magic ring. (6 sts)

Round 2: 2 sc in each st. (12 sts)

Round 3: *1 sc, 2 sc in the next st; rep from * to end. (18 sts)

Round 4: *2 sc, 2 sc in the next st; rep from * to end. (24 sts)

Round 5: *3 sc, 2 sc in the next st; rep from * to end. (30 sts)

Round 6: *4 sc, 2 sc in the next st; rep from * to end. (36 sts)

Round 7: *5 sc, 2 sc in the next st; rep from * to end. (42 sts)

Round 8: *13 sc, 2 sc in the next st; rep from * to end. (45 sts)

Rounds 9 to 16: 1 sc in each st.

Round 17: 1 slst, 1 sc, 1 hdc, 10 dc, 1 hdc, 1 sc, 1 slst, 1 sc, 1 hdc, 10 dc, 1 hdc, 1 sc, 1 slst, leave the rest of the stitches unworked.

Fasten off, leaving a long tail to sew to the head.

Ponytail

Round 1: Using **red**, ch 2, 4 sc in the second ch from hook. (4 sts)

Round 2: 1 sc in each st.

Round 3: 2 sc in each st. (8 sts)

Round 4: 1 sc in each st.

Round 5: 2 sc in the next 4 sts, 1 sc in the remaining 4 sts. (12 sts)

Round 6: *1 sc, 2 sc in the next st; rep from * to end. (18 sts)

Rounds 7 and 8: 1 sc in each st.

Round 9: *1 sc, sc2tog; rep from * to end. (12 sts)

Stuff firmly. Take the piece of wire and round both of its ends. Then insert the wire into the ponytail (*see Techniques: Inserting Wire Inside Certain Pieces*). You will be crocheting the rest of the ponytail with the wire inside.

Round 10: (sc2tog) 6 times. (6 sts)

Round 11: 1 sc in each st.

Round 12: 2 sc in each st. (12 sts)

Round 13: *1 sc, 2 sc in the next st; rep from * to end. (18 sts)

Rounds 14 to 18: 1 sc in each st.

Round 19: *1 sc, sc2tog; rep from * to end. (12 sts)

Stuff firmly surrounding the wire.

Round 20: (sc2tog) 6 times. (6 sts)

Round 21: 1 sc in each st.

Round 22: 2 sc in each st. (12 sts)

Round 23: *1 sc, 2 sc in the next st; rep from * to end. (18 sts)

Rounds 24 to 28: 1 sc in each st.

Round 29: *1 sc, sc2tog; rep from * to end. (12 sts)

Stuff firmly surrounding the wire.

Round 30: 1 sc in each st.

Round 31: Press the opening with your fingers, aligning 6 sts side by side and sc both sides together by working 1 sc into each pair of sts.

Fasten off, leaving a long tail to sew to the head.

TIP

If you are planning to crochet Scorpio for a little child, do not include the wire inside the ponytail.

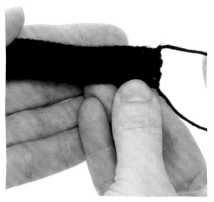

Bow

The bow is worked in rows.

Row 1: Using **black**, ch 25, 1 sc in the second ch from hook, 1 sc in each ch to end, ch 1, turn. (24 sts).

Rows 2 to 4: 1 sc BLO in each st, ch 1, turn.

Row 5: 1 sc BLO in each st.

Fasten off, leaving a long tail. Use this tail to sew both ends of this piece together, to form a ring. Weave in ends. Cut a length of black yarn, flatten the ring, wind the yarn around the middle of the work several times to create a bow. Once you are done, finish with a knot on the back of the bow, leaving a tail to sew it to the ponytail.

Shoes (Make Two)

Round 1: Using **black**, 5 sc in a magic ring. (5 sts)
Round 2: 2 sc in each st. (10 sts)
Round 3: *1 sc, 2 sc in the next st; rep from * to end. (15 sts)
Round 4: 1 sc BLO in each st
Rounds 5 and 6: 1 sc in each st.
Fasten off, leaving a long tail to sew to the leg.

Assembly

Sew the hair to the head (*see Techniques: Sewing the Hair*).
With the doll facing away from you, sew the ponytail to the back of the hair and slightly to the right.
Sew or tie the bow to the join between the hair and the ponytail.
Tie a bit of black yarn in each of the segments of the ponytail to enhance them.
Sew the shoes to the legs so they don't come off.
Sew the arms to the sides of the body (*see Techniques: Sewing the Arms*).
Weave in all ends inside the doll.

TIP

You can also crochet a pair of shoes using the same red yarn you used for the hair.

Yarn

100% 4-ply cotton; colours used: **skin** colour, **white**, **dark yellow**, **rose**, small amount of **pink**

Hooks

Size 2mm (US B/1) hook

Other Tools and Materials

Stitch marker

Safety eyes, 2 x 6mm (¼in)

Fibrefill stuffing

8 cm (3¼in) of coated craft wire

Finished size

15cm (6in) tall

Sagittarius

22 November-20 December

The 9th sign of the Zodiac

The future is full of potential and possibility and that's where Sagittarius is pointing her arrow! No one can discover new opportunities like true Sagittarians can - that's why they are so adventurous, optimistic and restless. Globetrotters to the core, these wanderers feel at home wherever they go. From trekking in South Africa to witnessing the Aurora Borealis, everything appeals to them. Ruled by upbeat Jupiter, Sagittarians tend to walk on the sunny roads of life and their happy-go-lucky attitude gains them friends from all over the world.

Symbol	Depiction	Element	Ruling Planet	Lucky Gemstone

Best Character Trait: Enthusiasm

Lucky Colour: Purple

Notable Sagittarius People: Jane Austen, Louisa May Alcott, Winston Churchill & Walt Disney

Makes Good Friends With: Gemini, Taurus & Aquarius

Leg 1

Round 1: Using **dark yellow** for sandals, 6 sc in a magic ring. (6 sts)
Round 2: 2 sc in each st. (12 sts)
Round 3: 1 sc BLO in each st.
Round 4: 1 sc in each st.
Round 5: Change to **skin** colour, 1 sc BLO in each st.
Rounds 6 to 10: 1 sc in each st.
Fasten off invisibly. Set aside.

Leg 2

Work as for Leg 1 to the end of round 10.
Round 11: Change to **white**, 1 sc BLO in each st.
Do not fasten off yarn. We will continue with the body.

Body

Still with leg 2 on your hook, ch 3 and join to leg 1 with a sc in the back look of any stitch of leg 1 (*see Techniques: Joining Legs – Option 1*). Work a further 11 sc through the back loops along leg 1.
Round 12: Place a stitch marker on the first stitch for new beg round, 1 sc into each ch of 3-ch-loop, 12 sc all along leg 2, 1 sc into other side of each ch of 3-ch-loop, 12 sc all along leg 1. (30 sts)
Rounds 13 to 17: 1 sc in each st.
Round 18: Change to **dark yellow**, 1 sc BLO in each st.
Round 19: *3 sc, sc2tog; rep from * to end. (24 sts)
Round 20: Change to **white**, 1 sc BLO in each st.
Rounds 21 and 22: 1 sc in each st.
Round 23: *2 sc, sc2tog; rep from * to end. (18 sts)
Stuff the body firmly at this point.
Rounds 24 and 25: 1 sc in each st.
Round 26: Change to **skin** colour, 1 sc BLO in each st
Round 27: *1 sc, sc2tog; rep from * to end. (12 sts)
Rounds 28 to 31: 1 sc in each st.
Do not fasten off yarn. We will continue with the head.

Head

Round 32: 2 sc in each st. (24 sts)
Round 33: *1 sc, 2 sc in the next st; rep from * to end. (36 sts)
Stuff the neck area firmly at this point.
Round 34: *5 sc, 2 sc in the next st; rep from * to end. (42 sts)
Rounds 35 and 36: 1 sc in each st.
Round 37: sc in each st until you are above the middle of the legs at the front of the body, 1 bobble st for the nose (*see Stitches: Bobble st*), sc in each st to end.
Rounds 38 to 47: 1 sc in each st.
Round 48: *5 sc, sc2tog; rep from * to end. (36 sts)
Place the safety eyes one round above the nose, with 8 sts between them, embroider cheeks with **pink** yarn.
Round 49: *4 sc, sc2tog; rep from * to end. (30 sts)
Round 50: *3 sc, sc2tog; rep from * to end. (24 sts)
Start stuffing the head at this point.
Round 51: *2 sc, sc2tog; rep from * to end. (18 sts)
Round 52: *1 sc, sc2tog; rep from * to end. (12 sts)
Stuff firmly.
Round 53: (sc2tog) 6 times. (6 sts)
Fasten off and weave in ends.

TIP

Sew the hair first and then the ears, in line with the nose! It will make their placement easier if the hair is sewn first.

Arms (Make Two)

Round 1: Using **skin** colour, ch 2, 4 sc in the second ch from hook. (4 sts)
Round 2: 2 sc in each st. (8 sts)
Rounds 3 to 5: 1 sc in each st.
Round 6: Change to **dark yellow**, 1 sc BLO in each st.
Rounds 7 and 8: 1 sc in each st.
Round 9: Change to **skin colour**, 1 sc BLO in each st.
Rounds 11 to 16: 1 sc in each st.
Round 17: Press the opening with your fingers, aligning 4 sts side by side and sc both sides together by working 1 sc into each pair of sts (*see Techniques: Closing the Arms*).
Fasten off, leaving a long tail to sew to the body.

Ears (Make Two)

Round 1: Using **skin** colour, 6 sc in a magic ring. (6 sts)
Close the ring with a sl st into the first sc and fasten off, leaving a long tail to sew to the head.

Skirt

Turn the body upside down and join **white** yarn into one of the front loops of round 18, at the back of the body.
Round 1: 1 sc in FLO of each st of round 18. (30 sts)
Round 2: *4 sc, 2 sc in the next st; rep from * to end. (36 sts)
Round 3: 1 sc in each st.
Round 4: *5 sc, 2 sc in the next st; rep from * to end. (42 sts)
Round 5: 1 sc in each st.
Round 6: 1 sc in the first 3 sts, 2 sc in the next st, *6 sc, 2 sc in the next st; rep from * 4 more times, 1 sc in the last 3 sts. (48 sts)
Rounds 7 and 8: 1 sc in each st.
Fasten off and weave in ends.

Hair

Round 1: Using **rose**, 6 sc in a magic ring. (6 sts)
Round 2: *2 sc in each st, rep from * to end. (12 sts)
Round 3: *1 sc, 2 sc in the next st; rep from * to end. (18 sts)
Round 4: *2 sc, 2 sc in the next st; rep from * to end. (24 sts)
Round 5: *3 sc, 2 sc in the next st; rep from * to end. (30 sts)
Round 6: *4 sc, 2 sc in the next st; rep from * to end. (36 sts)
Round 7: *5 sc, 2 sc in the next st; rep from * to end. (42 sts)
Round 8: *13 sc, 2 sc in the next st; rep from * to end. (45 sts)
Rounds 9 to 16: 1 sc in each st.
Round 17: 1 slst, * ch 36, 1 sc in second ch from hook, 1 sc in each st along ch (35 sts), 1 slst; rep from * once more, leaving the rest of the stitches in the round unworked.
Fasten off, leaving a long tail to sew to the head.

Hairbun

Round 1: Using **rose**, 5 sc in a magic ring. (5 sts)
Round 2: 2 sc in each st. (10 sts)
Round 3: *1 sc, 2 sc in the next st; rep from * to end. (15 sts)
Round 4: *2 sc, 2 sc in the next st; rep from * to end. (20 sts)
Rounds 5 to 7: 1 sc in each st.
Round 8: *2 sc, sc2tog; rep from * to end. (15 sts)
Round 9: 1 sc in each st.
Fasten off, leaving a long tail to sew.

TIP

When sewing the hair, make sure you place it so that the two long hairlocks sit right in the middle of the forehead and part them along each side of the head.

Bow

Round 1: Using **dark yellow**, ch 2, 4 sc in the second ch from hook. (4 sts)
Round 2: *1 sc, 2 sc in the next st; rep from * to end. (6 sts)
Rounds 3 to 30: 1 sc in each st
No need to stuff. Take the piece of wire and round both of the ends (*see Techniques: Inserting Wire Inside Certain Pieces*), then insert it inside the tube. Close the tube through the front loops. Fasten off, leaving a long tail (*see Techniques: Closing Remaining Stitches through the Front Loops*).

Assembly

Sew the hair to the head (*see Techniques: Sewing the Hair*), with the two long locks on the forehead.
Sew the ears to the sides of the head. Then part the two hairlocks, one to each side, and secure them with some stitches to the back of the ear.
Stuff and sew the hair-bun to the head, then wrap it with a bit of **dark yellow** yarn.
Sew the arms to the sides of the body (*see Techniques: Sewing the Arms*).
Use a small amount of **dark yellow** yarn to add laces to the sandals and wrap them around the legs.
Shape the bow and, with your tapestry needle, pass the remaining tail through the hand and sew it to the other end of the bow.
Weave in all ends inside the doll.

TIP

If you are planning to crochet a Sagittarius doll for a little child do not include the wire inside the bow. Just stuff it slightly.

Yarn

100 % 4-ply cotton; colours used: **skin** colour, **purple**, **white**, **dark grey**, **lilac**, **dark yellow**, a small amount of **pink**

Hooks

Size 2mm (US B/1) hook

Other Tools and Materials

Stitch marker

Safety eyes, 2 x 6mm (¼in)

Fibrefill stuffing

Coated wire, 2 pieces x 5cm (2in)

Round-nosed pliers

Finished size

19cm (7½in) tall

Capricorn

21 December-19 January
The 10th sign of the Zodiac

Industrious Capricorns are one of the most organized and reliable signs of the Zodiac. Patiently and steadily, they know how to work hard to achieve their aims, especially those which they have planned with much anticipation. Ruled by serious Saturn, Capricorn characters usually have control over their emotions, but once you get to know them, they can have an amusing sense of humour. They will surely surprise you! But do not expect them to not play by the rules. This is one of the most conservative signs of all and they love it.

Symbol	Depiction	Element	Ruling Planet	Lucky Gemstone

Best Character Trait: Determination

Lucky Colour: Brown

Notable Capricorn People: Isaac Newton, Dolly Parton, Martin Luther King Jr. & Catherine, the Duchess of Cambridge

Makes Good Friends With: Virgo, Taurus & Scorpio

Body

Round 1: Using **lilac**, 6 sc in a magic ring. (6 sts)

Round 2: 1 sc in each st.

Round 3: 2 sc in each st. (12 sts)

Rounds 4 and 5: 1 sc in each st.

Round 6: *1 sc, 2 sc in the next st; rep from * to end. (18 sts)

Rounds 7 and 8: 1 sc in each st.

Round 9: *2 sc, 2 sc in the next st; rep from * to end. (24 sts)

Round 10: 1 sc in each st.

Round 11: 1 sc BLO sc in each st.

Round 12: *3 sc, 2 sc in the next st; rep from * to end. (30 sts)

Round 13: 1 sc BLO sc in each st

Round 14: 1 sc in each st.

Round 15: 1 sc BLO sc in each st.

Round 16: 1 sc in each st.

Round 17: 1 sc BLO in each st.

Round 18: *3 sc, sc2tog; rep from * to end. (24 sts)

Round 19: Change to **white**, 1 sc BLO in each st.

Round 20: 1 sc in each st.

Round 21: Change to **dark grey**, 1 sc in each st.

Round 22: *2 sc, sc2tog; rep from * to end. (18 sts)
Stuff the body firmly at this point.

Round 23: Change to **white**, 1 sc in each st.

Round 24: 1 sc in each st.

Round 25: Change to **dark grey**, 1 sc in each st.

Round 26: *1 sc, sc2tog; rep from * to end. (12 sts)

Round 27: Change to **white**, 1 sc in each st.

Round 28: 1 sc in each st.

Round 29: Change to **dark grey**, 1 sc in each st.

Round 30: 1 sc in each st.

Round 31: Change to **skin** colour, 1 sc BLO in each st.
Do not fasten off yarn. We will continue with the head.

Head

Round 32: 2 sc in each st. (24 sts)

Round 33: *1 sc, 2 sc in the next st; rep from * to end. (36 sts)
Stuff the neck area firmly at this point.

Round 34: *5 sc, 2 sc in the next st; rep from * to end. (42 sts)

Rounds 35 and 36: 1 sc in each st.

Round 37: sc in each st until you are above the middle of the legs at the front of the body, 1 bobble st for the nose (*see Stitches: Bobble st*), sc in each st to end.

Rounds 38 to 47: 1 sc in each st.

Round 48: *5 sc, sc2tog; rep from * to end. (36 sts)
Place safety eyes one round above the nose, with 8 sts between them, embroider cheeks with **pink** yarn.

Round 49: *4 sc, sc2tog; rep from * to end. (30 sts)

Round 50: *3 sc, sc2tog; rep from * to end. (24 sts)
Start stuffing the head at this point.

Round 51: *2 sc, sc2tog; rep from * to end. (18 sts)

Round 52: *1 sc, sc2tog; rep from * to end. (12 sts)
Stuff firmly.

Round 53: (sc2tog) 6 times. (6 sts)
Fasten off and weave in ends

Scales

Turn the body upside down and join **lilac** yarn in one of the front loops of round 19, at the back of the body.

You'll be working continuously on the spiral of remaining front loops from round 19 to round 11: *2 sl st, (1 hdc, 3 dc, 1 hdc) all in the next st; rep from * to end. (46 scales)

Fins (Make Two)

Round 1: Using **lilac**, 6 sc in a magic ring. (6 sts)

Round 2: 1 sc in each st.

Round 3: 2 sc in each st. (12 sts)

Rounds 4 and 5: 1 sc in each st.

Round 6: *1 sc, 2 sc in the next st; rep from * to end. (18 sts)

Rounds 7 and 8: 1 sc in each st.

Round 9: *1 sc, sc2tog; rep from * to end. (12 sts)

No need to stuff.

Rounds 10 and 11: 1 sc in each st.

Round 12: (sc2tog) 6 times. (6 sts)

Fasten off, leaving a long tail to sew to the tip of the fish tail.

TIP

Do not stuff the fins and remember to flatten them into shape!

TIP

Capricorn's hair locks should curl as you go. If they don't, help them into shape by twisting them with your fingers.

Arms (Make Two)

Round 1: Using **skin** colour, ch 2, 4 sc in the second ch from hook. (4 sts)
Round 2: 2 sc in each st. (8 sts)
Rounds 3 to 16: 1 sc in each st.
Round 17: Press the opening with your fingers, aligning 4 sts side by side and sc both sides together by working 1 sc into each pair of sts (*see Techniques: Closing the Arms*).
Fasten off, leaving a long tail to sew to the body.

Hair

Round 1: Using **purple**, 6 sc in a magic ring. (6 sts)
Round 2: 2 sc in each st. (12 sts)
Round 3: *1 sc, 2 sc in the next st; rep from * to end. (18 sts)
Round 4: *2 sc, 2 sc in the next st; rep from * to end. (24 sts)
Round 5: *3 sc, 2 sc in the next st; rep from * to end. (30 sts)
Round 6: *4 sc, 2 sc in the next st; rep from * to end. (36 sts)
Round 7: *5 sc, 2 sc in the next st; rep from * to end. (42 sts)
Round 8: *13 sc, 2 sc in the next st; rep from * to end. (45 sts)
Rounds 9 to 16: 1 sc in each st.
Round 17: * ch 9, 1 sc in second ch from hook, 1 sc in each st along ch (8 sts), 2 sc, rep from * to create 14 short hair locks,** ch 21, 1 sc in second ch from hook, 1 sc in each st along ch (20 sts), 1 sc, rep from ** to create 17 long hair locks.
Fasten off, leaving a long tail to sew to the head.

Horns (Make Two)

Round 1: Using **dark yellow** colour, ch 2, 4 sc in the second ch from hook. (4 sts)

Round 2: *1 sc, 2 sc in the next st; rep from * to end. (6 sts)

Round 3: 1 sc in each st.

Round 4: *2 sc, 2 sc in the next st; rep from * to end. (8 sts)

Round 5: 1 sc BLO in each st.

Round 6: 1 sc in each st.

Round 7: 1 sc BLO in each st.

Round 8: 1 sc in each st.

Round 9: 1 sc BLO in each st.

Round 10: 1 sc in each st.

Round 11: 1 sc BLO in each st.

Round 12: 1 sc in each st.

Round 13: 1 sc BLO in each st.

Round 14: 1 sc in each st.

Round 15: 1 sc BLO in each st.

Round 16: 1 sc in each st.

Fasten off, leaving a long tail to sew to the head.

Assembly

Sew the hair to the head (*see Techniques: Sewing the Hair*).

Sew the arms to the sides of the body (*see Techniques: Sewing the Arms*).

Round the ends of the pieces of coated wire into loops and place them inside the horns. Stuff them slightly and sew them to the hair. Then curve them slightly backwards.

Sew the fins to the tip of Capricorn's tail.

Weave in all ends inside the doll.

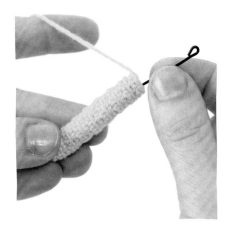

TIP

If you are planning to crochet a Capricorn doll for a little child, do not include the wire inside the horns. Just stuff them and curve them slightly.

Yarn

100% 4-ply cotton; colours used: **skin** colour, **white**, **dark grey**, **baby blue**, **blue**, **dark rose**, small amount of **pink**

Hooks

Size 2mm (US B/1) hook

Other Tools and Materials

Stitch marker

Safety eyes, 2 x 6mm (¼in)

Fibrefill stuffing

Finished size:

15cm (6in) tall.

Aquarius

20 January-17 February

The 11ᵗʰ sign of the Zodiac

You can trust an Aquarian friend to be there for you! People born under this sign are all about social justice and the well-being of others, they make the best humanitarians. Insatiably curious, eccentric and original, Aquarius is often the leader of innovative change, so no wonder they find science and technology very interesting. Ruled by rebellious Uranus, they can also be a bit quirky but they were born to make friends and, even though they are highly independent, they love to be part of a group.

Symbol	Depiction	Element	Ruling Planet	Lucky Gemstone

Best Character Trait: Ingenuity

Lucky Colour: Blue

Notable Aquarius People: Wolfgang Amadeus Mozart, Charles Darwin, Rosa Parks & Oprah Winfrey

Makes Good Friends With: Libra, Gemini & Sagittarius

Leg 1

Round 1: Using **skin** colour, 6 sc in a magic ring. (6 sts)
Round 2: 2 sc in each st. (12 sts)
Round 3: 1 sc BLO in each st.
Rounds 4 to 10: 1 sc in each st.
Fasten off invisibly. Set aside.

Leg 2

Work as for Leg 1 the end of round 10.
Round 11: Change to **white**, 1 sc BLO in each st.
Do not fasten off yarn. We will continue with the body.

Body

Still with leg 2 on your hook, ch 3 and join to leg 1 with a sc in the back loop of any stitch of leg 1 (*see Techniques: Joining Legs – Option 1*). Work a further 11 sc through the back loops along leg 1.
Round 12: Place a stitch marker on the first stitch for the beg of round, 1 sc into each ch of 3-ch-loop, 12 sc all along leg 2, 1 sc into other side of each ch of 3-ch-loop, 12 sc all along leg 1. (30 sts)
Rounds 13 to 17: 1 sc in each st.
Round 18: Change to **dark grey**, 1 sc BLO in each st.
Round 19: *3 sc, sc2tog; rep from * to end. (24 sts)
Rounds 20 to 22: 1 sc in each st.
Round 23: *2 sc, sc2tog; rep from * to end. (18 sts)
Stuff the body firmly at this point.
Rounds 24 to 26: 1 sc in each st.
Round 27: *1 sc, sc2tog; rep from * to end. (12 sts)
Rounds 28 to 30: 1 sc in each st.
Round 31: Change to **skin** colour, 1 sc BLO in each st.
Do not fasten off yarn. We will continue with the head.

Head

Round 32: 2 sc in each st. (24 sts)
Round 33: *1 sc, 2 sc in the next st; rep from * to end. (36 sts)
Stuff the neck area firmly at this point.
Round 34: *5 sc, 2 sc in the next st; rep from * to end. (42 sts)
Rounds 35 and 36: 1 sc in each st.
Round 37: sc in each st until you are above the middle of the legs at the front of the body, 1 bobble st for the nose (*see Stitches: Bobble st*), sc in each st to end.
Rounds 38 to 47: 1 sc in each st.
Round 48: *5 sc, sc2tog; rep from * to end. (36 sts)
Place safety eyes one round above the nose, with 8 sts between them, embroider cheeks with **pink** yarn.
Round 49: *4 sc, sc2tog; rep from * to end. (30 sts)
Round 50: *3 sc, sc2tog; rep from * to end. (24 sts)
Start stuffing the head at this point.
Round 51: *2 sc, sc2tog; rep from * to end. (18 sts)
Round 52: *1 sc, sc2tog; rep from * to end. (12 sts)
Stuff firmly.
Round 53: (sc2tog) 6 times. (6 sts)
Fasten off and weave in ends.

Arms (Make Two)

Round 1: Using **skin** colour, ch 2, 4 sc in the second ch from hook. (4 sts)

Round 2: 2 sc in each st. (8 sts)

Rounds 3 to 16: 1 sc in each st.

Round 17: Press the opening with your fingers, aligning 4 sts side by side and sc both sides together by working 1 sc into each pair of sts (*see Techniques: Closing the Arms*).

Fasten off, leaving a long tail to sew to the body.

Hair

Round 1: Using **baby blue**, 6 sc in a magic ring. (6 sts)

Round 2: 2 sc in each st. (12 sts)

Round 3: *1 sc, 2 sc in the next st; rep from * to end. (18 sts)

Round 4: *2 sc, 2 sc in the next st; rep from * to end. (24 sts)

Round 5: *3 sc, 2 sc in the next st; rep from * to end. (30 sts)

Round 6: *4 sc, 2 sc in the next st; rep from * to end. (36 sts)

Round 7: *5 sc, 2 sc in the next st; rep from * to end. (42 sts)

Round 8: *13 sc, 2 sc in the next st; rep from * to end. (45 sts)

Rounds 9 to 16: 1 sc in each st.

Round 17: 1 slst, * ch 31, 1 sc in second ch from hook, 1 sc in each st along ch (30 sts), 1 slst; rep from * twice more, in the same stitch, 16 sc, 1 slst, ** ch 41, 1 sc in second ch from hook, 1 sc in each st along ch (40 sts), 1 slst; rep from ** 3 times more, in the same stitch, 16 sc, 1 slst, ***ch 31, 1 sc in second ch from hook, 1 sc in each st along ch (30 sts), 1 slst; rep from *** twice more, in the same stitch.

Fasten off, leaving a long tail to sew to the head.

TIP

You won't need to sew the long locks. Just place two on each side and tie them to the others to create the ponytails.

Shorts

Leg 1
Round 1: Using **blue**, ch 20, 1 sc in the first chain (the 20th chain from hook) to form a ring, 1 sc in each st along ch. (20 sts)
Round 2: 1 sc in each st.
Fasten off invisibly and weave in ends. Set aside.

Leg 2
Work as for Leg 1 but do not fasten off.
We will start with the main body of the shorts.
Round 3: Still with leg 2 on your hook, ch 2 and join to leg 1 with a sc in any stitch of leg 1. Place a stitch marker on this first stitch for beg of round, work 19 sc along leg 1, 1 sc into each ch of 2-ch-loop, 20 sc all along leg 2, 1 sc into other side of each ch of 2-ch-loop. (44 sts)
Round 4: *20 sc, sc2tog; rep from * once more. (42 sts)
Round 5: *5 sc, sc2tog; rep from * to end. (36 sts)
Round 6: 1 sc in each st.

Round 7: *4 sc, sc2tog; rep from * to end. (30 sts)
Rounds 8 to 9: 1 sc in each st.
Round 10: 1 sc BLO in each st.
Round 11: 1 sc in each st.
Fasten off and weave in ends.

Suspender
Row 1: Using **blue** and leaving a long initial tail, ch 22.
Fasten off, leaving a long tail.

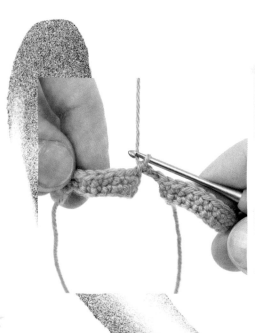

TIP

Don't forget to fully stuff the urn before closing it completely with the water lid.

Urn

Water lid

Round 1: Using 2mm hook and **baby blue** for the water lid, 6 sc in a magic ring. (6 sts)
Round 2: 2 sc in each st to end. (12 sts)
Fasten off invisibly and weave in ends. Set aside.

Urn

Round 1: Using **dark rose**, 6 sc in a magic ring. (6 sts)
Round 2: 2 sc in each st to end. (12 sts)
Round 3: 2 sc in each st to end. (24 sts)
Round 4: 1 sc BLO in each st.
Rounds 5 to 6: 1 sc in each st.
Round 7: *3 sc, 2 sc in the next st; rep from * to end. (30 sts)
Rounds 8 to 14: 1 sc in each st.
Round 15: *3 sc, sc2tog; rep from * to end. (24 sts)
Round 16: *2 sc, sc2tog; rep from * to end. (18 sts)
Start stuffing the urn at this point.
Round 17: *1 sc, sc2tog; rep from * to end. (12 sts)
Rounds 18 to 20: 1 sc in each st.
Place the water lid over the opening of the urn.
Round 21: 1 sc joining one st of the opening of the urn with one st of the water lid.
Round 22: 2 sc in each st to end. (24 sts)
Round 23: *3 sc, 2 sc in the next st; rep from * to end. (30 sts)
Round 24: 1 slst in each st.
Fasten off and weave in ends.

Assembly

Sew the hair to the head (*see Techniques: Sewing the Hair*), with the four long hairlocks over the forehead. Divide the hairlocks in half, securing the two hairlocks of each side near each of the ponytails by tying them all together with bit of dark grey yarn.
Pull the shorts over the legs.
Sew the suspender, crossed from front to back, using the two remaining yarn tails.
Weave in all ends inside the doll.

Yarn

100% 4-ply cotton; colours used: **skin** colour, **light turquoise, light green, white, light pink, pink**

40% Acrylic, 30% Mohair, 30% Polyamide, 1 ply; colour used: **white**

Hooks

Size 2mm (US B/1) hook

Other Tools and Materials

Stitch marker

Safety eyes, 4 x 6mm (¼in)

Fibrefill stuffing

Finished size

23cm (9in) tall

Pisces

18 February-19 March
The 12ᵗʰ sign of the Zodiac

Like fish in gentle waters, Pisceans love to bask in a world of myths, fantasies and dreams. Their imagination knows no limits so they are one of the most naturally creative signs of the Zodiac and the best of storytellers. We must thank their ruling planet Neptune for all these skills. Compassionate, devoted and emphatic, Pisces can feel what everyone is feeling (when they say 'I know how you feel', they truly mean it!) and can easily read the mood of any party or gathering. This renders Pisceans as the most attentive of friends, putting the needs of others before their very own.

Symbol	Depiction	Element	Ruling Planet	Lucky Gemstone

Best Character Trait: Empathy
Lucky Colour: Turquoise
Notable Pisces People: Albert Einstein, Ruth Bader Ginsburg, Steve Jobs & Simone Biles
Makes Good Friends With: Cancer, Scorpio & Taurus

Body

Round 1: Using **light turquoise** for doll 1 or **light green** for doll 2, ch 2, 4 sc in the second ch from hook. (4 sts)

Round 2: *1 sc, 2 sc in the next st; rep from * to end. (6 sts)

Round 3: *2 sc, 2 sc in the next st; rep from * to end. (8 sts)

Round 4: *1 sc, 2 sc in the next st; rep from * to end. (12 sts)

Rounds 5 and 6: 1 sc in each st.

Round 7: *1 sc, 2 sc in the next st; rep from * to end. (18 sts)

Round 8: 1 sc in the next 8 sts, 2 sc in the following 2 sts, 1 sc in the remaining 8 sts (20 sts)

Round 9: 1 sc in the next 9 sts, *2 sc in the next st, 1 sc in the next st; rep from * once more, sc in the remaining 7 sts (22 sts)

Round 10: 1 sc in the next 10 sts, 2 sc in the next st, 1 sc in the next 2 sts, 2 sc in the next st, 1 sc in the remaining 8 sts (24 sts)

Round 11: 1 sc in the next 7 sts, *2 sc in the next st, 1 sc in the next st; rep from * once more, 2 sc in the next stitch, **1 sc in the next st, 2 sc in the next st; rep from ** twice more, 1 sc in the remaining 6 sts. (30 sts)

Rounds 12 to 17: 1 sc in each st.

Round 18: 1 sc in next 10 sts. Move the stitch marker to the last st, this will now mark the beginning of the round. Leave the rest of the sts in this round unworked.

Round 19: Change to **skin** colour, 1 sc BLO in each st.

Round 20: *3 sc, sc2tog; rep from * to end. (24 sts)

Rounds 21 and 22: 1 sc in each st.

Stuff the body firmly at this point.

Round 23: Change to **white**, 1 sc BLO in each st.

Round 24: *2 sc, sc2tog; rep from * to end. (18 sts)

Rounds 25 to 27: 1 sc in each st.

Round 28: Change to **skin** colour, 1 sc BLO in each st.

Round 29: *1 sc, sc2tog; rep from * to end. (12 sts)

Rounds 30 to 33: 1 sc in each st.

Do not fasten off yarn. We will continue with the head.

Head

Round 34: 2 sc in each st. (24 sts)

Round 35: *1 sc, 2 sc in the next st; rep from * to end. (36 sts)

Stuff the neck area firmly at this point.

Round 36: *5 sc, 2 sc in the next st; rep from * to end. (42 sts)

Rounds 37 and 38: 1 sc in each st.

Round 39: sc in each st until you are above the middle of the legs at the front of the body, 1 bobble st for the nose (*see Stitches: Bobble st*), sc in each st to end.

Rounds 40 to 49: 1 sc in each st.

Round 50: *5 sc, sc2tog; rep from * to end. (36 sts)

Place safety eyes one round above the nose, with 8 sts between them, embroider cheeks with **pink** yarn.

Round 51: *4 sc, sc2tog; rep from * to end. (30 sts)

Round 52: *3 sc, sc2tog; rep from * to end. (24 sts)

Start stuffing the head at this point.

Round 53: *2 sc, sc2tog; rep from * to end. (18 sts)

Round 54: *1 sc, sc2tog; rep from * to end. (12 sts)

Stuff firmly.

Round 55: (sc2tog) 6 times. (6 sts)

Fasten off and weave in ends.

Ruffle of the Fish Tail

Turn the body upside down and join **light turquoise** yarn for doll 1 or **light green** yarn for doll 2 in one of the front loops of round 19, at the back of the doll.

Round 1: 1 sc in each st. (30 sts)

Round 2: 2 sc in each st. (60 sts)

Round 3: 2 sc in each st. (120 sts)

Fasten off and weave in ends.

TIP

Arrange the ruffle with your fingers, giving shape to the waves so they undulate up and down.

Fins (Make Two)

Round 1: Using **light turquoise** for doll 1 or **light green** for doll 2, 6 sc in a magic ring. (6 sts)

Round 2: 1 sc in each st.

Round 3: 2 sc in each st. (12 sts)

Rounds 4 and 5: 1 sc in each st.

Round 6: *1 sc, 2 sc in the next st; rep from * to end. (18 sts)

Rounds 7 and 8: 1 sc in each st.

Round 9: *1 sc, sc2tog; rep from * to end. (12 sts)

No need to stuff.

Rounds 10 and 11: 1 sc in each st.

Round 12: (sc2tog) 6 times. (6 sts)

Fasten off, leaving a long tail to sew to the tip of the fish tail.

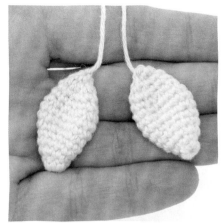

Arms (Make Two)

Round 1: Using **skin** colour, ch 2, 4 sc in the second ch from hook. (4 sts)

Round 2: 2 sc in each st. (8 sts)

Rounds 3 to 16: 1 sc in each st.

Round 17: Press the opening with your fingers, aligning 4 sts side by side and sc both sides together by working 1 sc into each pair of sts (*see Techniques: Closing the Arms*).

Fasten off, leaving a long tail to sew to the body.

Strap of the Top

Row 1: Using **white** and leaving a long initial tail, ch 17.

Fasten off, leaving a long tail to sew around the neck.

TIP

Do not stuff the fins and remember to flatten them into shape!

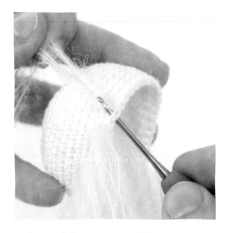

Hair Cap

Round 1: Using **white**, 6 sc in a magic ring. (6 sts)
Round 2: 2 sc in each st. (12 sts)
Round 3: *1 sc, 2 sc in the next st; rep from * to end. (18 sts)
Round 4: *2 sc, 2 sc in the next st; rep from * to end. (24 sts)
Round 5: *3 sc, 2 sc in the next st; rep from * to end. (30 sts)
Round 6: *4 sc, 2 sc in the next st; rep from * to end. (36 sts)
Round 7: *5 sc, 2 sc in the next st; rep from * to end. (42 sts)
Round 8: *13 sc, 2 sc in the next st; rep from * to end. (45 sts)
Rounds 9 to 17: 1 sc in each st.
Fasten off, leaving a long tail to sew to the head.

Hair

Cut 180 pieces of **white** mohair yarn, approximately 20 cm long, to pass through each stitch along the opening of the hair cap. Take 4 pieces and pass them through one stitch, folding them in half. Repeat this for all stitches in the round. Set aside.

TIP

If you'd rather not use Mohair yarn for your Pisces doll, Virgo's and Leo's hair are pretty good options too!

Star (make one in light pink and one in pink)

Round 1: 5 sc in a magic ring. (5 sts)
Round 2: 2 sc in each st. (10 sts)
Round 3: *1 sc, 2 sc in the next st; rep from * to end. (15 sts)
Round 4: *(1 sc, 1 hdc, 1 dc, 1 hdc, 1 sc) all in the next st, 2 slst; rep from * to end.
Fasten off, leaving a long tail to tie to the hair.

Assembly

Sew the hair cap to the head (*see Techniques: Sewing the Hair*), then tie the hair into a high ponytail with a length of pink yarn. Trim to the desired length.
Using the remaining yarn tails, sew the stars to the ponytail.
Sew the arms to the sides of the body (*see Techniques: Sewing the Arms*).
Sew the strap to the centre of the top, wrap it around the neck and join in the same place of the top.
Sew the fins to the tip of the tail.
Weave in all ends inside the doll.

TIP

If you want your Pisces mermaids to have another hair colour, remember that the hair cap should always be made with a similar colour to the Mohair yarn of your choice.

Techniques and Tutorials

Anatomy of a Stitch

Every finished stitch looks like a sideways letter **v**, with two loops meeting at one end (**1**). The loop closer to you is the **front loop** and the loop behind it is the **back loop**. You will sometimes be asked to crochet certain stitches in the front loops (FLO) or in the back loops (BLO) only and there's always a reason for this: you will use the remaining loops later!

Increasing

This means working two stitches in the same stitch (**2**). After you have worked the first stitch, you simply insert your hook back into the same place and work the next stitch.

Invisible Single Crochet Decrease

A crochet decrease means working two stitches together at the same time into one stitch. For the patterns in this book it is better to use the invisible single crochet decrease, so that it goes unnoticed. Insert the hook in the front loop of the next stitch (**3**) and in the front loop of the stitch next to that, one at a time (**4**). Yarn over hook and draw it through the first two loops on your hook. Yarn over hook again and draw it through the two remaining loops on your hook (**5**).

TIP

An invisible single crochet decrease can be used to make your decreasing less visible by working only into the front loops of the stitches being worked.

Changing Colour

To change to another colour you should join the new colour during the final step of the last stitch in the previous colour. This means that when the last two loops of the stitch remain on your hook (**1**), you should grab the new colour, wrap it around your hook (**2**) and pull it through those two loops. This will leave the new colour on your hook (**3**), ready to work the next stitch in that colour (**4**).

All colour changes in this book are made into pieces that will be stuffed later, so cut the old colour yarn and tie this into a knot with the new colour yarn, inside the piece, to secure both tails.

Fasten Off Invisibly

This method avoids the little stub that can look unsightly when you fasten off your crochet. When you have your final loop on hook and have finished your crochet, cut yarn, take yarn over hook and pull all the way through final loop. Pull yarn tight, which creates a small knot. Thread yarn tail onto tapestry needle and insert needle, from back of work, underneath the top **v** of second stitch along the main edge (**5**). Pull yarn all the way through. Insert needle from front, into the top **v** of the last stitch made and pull yarn through (**6**). You have created a 'mimic' stitch that covers the small knot and joins up the round neatly.

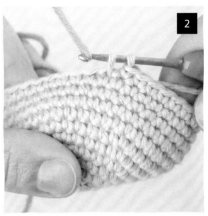
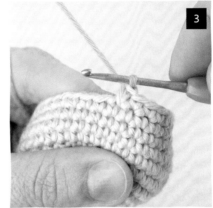

Closing Remaining Stitches through the Front Loops

After the final round, you may be instructed to close the remaining stitches through the front loops. To do this, fasten off after last stitch and thread yarn onto a tapestry needle. Insert needle through each visible loop of the last round of stitches (through one loop of stitch only) (**1**). When you reach the end, pull gently to close up the gap (**2**). Secure the thread with a few stitches and hide the ends inside the doll.

Hiding Ends Inside the Doll

Insert your crochet hook into the doll, in between stitches, a few centimetres (a couple of inches) from the tail end that you want to hide, then push the hook out between stitches that are close to the tail end, making sure that the hook is really close to the tail end of yarn (**3**). Take yarn over hook and pull through the doll and as you pull out your hook, the yarn will come with it. Snip the yarn close to the doll to leave a clean finish (**4**).

Working in Rows

Flat pieces are worked in rows, starting with a foundation chain. This is a string of chain stitches. It's important not to twist the chain, so keep a tight grip on the crocheted chains near your hook.

Working in Rounds

All the dolls in this book are worked in rounds, in a continuous spiral, so there's no need to close the round after finishing each one of them. This is why the use of stitch markers is essential. It's important to mark the beginning of each round with a stitch marker and move this stitch marker up as you work.

Magic Ring

Round pieces always start with a magic ring, because, when tightened, it will leave no holes in the middle where stuffing could come out. To make a magic ring, start in the same way that you would a slip knot, by making a loop shape with the tail end of the yarn. Insert the hook into it and draw another loop of yarn through it. But do not pull the tail end. As well as the loop on your hook, you will have a large loop sitting beneath your hook, with a twisted section of yarn (**1**). It is important that you work into the centre of the loop for your first round, and also that you work over the twisted section of yarn (**2**). When you have completed your first round, you can pull the yarn tail tight to close the hole (**3**).

TIP

All the dolls are worked in rounds, in a continuous spiral, so it is essential to use a stitch marker to help identify the beginning of each round. Move the stitch marker up as you work.

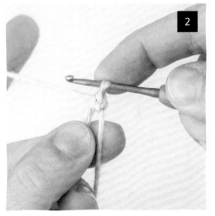

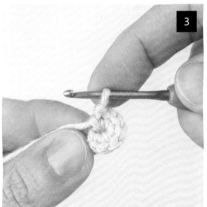

TIP

You may need to practise a few times before you feel totally comfortable with the technique, but if you can persevere and master it, the start of your crochet will be really neat.

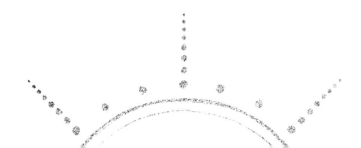

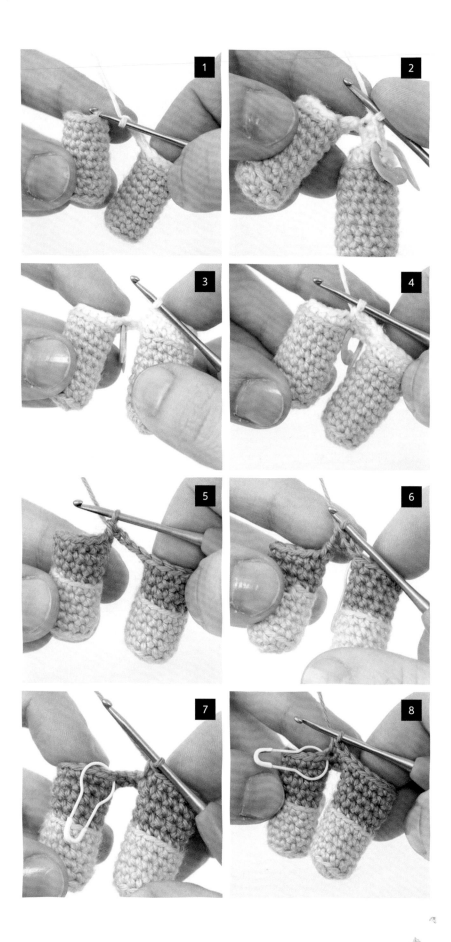

Joining Legs

Except for Pisces and Capricorn, you will begin all other dolls in this book by crocheting the legs, which need to be joined, then continue with the body up to the head. There are two ways to do this, depending on if the doll is wearing underwear or trousers. In both cases you will crochet one leg first and set it aside while you crochet the second leg.

Option 1 (with underwear): with leg 2 still on your hook, you will chain 3 to join leg 1 with a sc into any back loop of leg 1 (**1**). You will then crochet a further 11 sc BLO all along leg 1. This will be the new beginning of the following rounds so it's important to place a stitch marker on the first stitch you are about to make. Crochet 3 sc into one of the sides of the 3-ch-loop (**2**). Then, crochet 12 sc along leg 2 (**3**) so you can finally work 3 sc on the other side of the 3-ch-loop (**4**). You will end up with a round of 30 stitches which will be the beginning of the body of your doll.

Option 2 (with trousers): with leg 2 still on your hook, you will chain 3 to join leg 1 with a sc (**5**). This will be the new beginning of the following rounds, so it's important to place a stitch marker here. You will then have to crochet a further 11 sc all along leg 1 and, after that, crochet 3 sc in one of the sides of the 3-ch-loop (**6**). Then, crochet 12 sc along leg 2 (**7**) so you can finally work 3 sc on the other side of the 3-ch-loop (**8**). You will end up with a round of 30 stitches which will be the beginning of the body of your doll.

Interrupting your Work

Sometimes I will recommend you to stop crocheting the head at some point before finishing, either to crochet a dress or collar without having the stuffed head interfering with the movements of your hands. To do this, you can place a stitch marker on the loop on your hook, so the stitches won't come off (**1**). Then you can cut the yarn (**2**). When you are ready, you can join the yarn again as you would do for a colour change.

 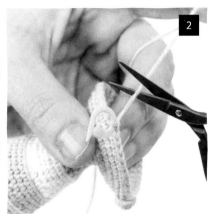

Attaching Eyes

Safety eyes have two parts: the front with a straight or threaded rod, and a washer that goes inside the toy. If fastened correctly, it's almost impossible to remove them. For extra precaution, you can add a tiny bit of craft glue to the washer. But beware, if you are crocheting the doll for a small child, you should probably consider embroidering the eyes using **black, dark grey** or **brown** leftover pieces of yarn.

TIP

Remember to always place your doll head downwards when joining the yarn to create a skirt or collar!

Sewing the Cheeks

These are made whilst the head is in progress, after you have attached the safety eyes (if using). Use a short length of **pink** yarn and thread onto a tapestry needle. Working from the inside of the head, in line with lower edge of eye and a few stitches away, make a small running stitch over two stitches, in a straight line (**1**), bringing needle back through to inside of head. If you want the cheek to be thicker, do this twice. Tie off ends inside the head.

Weaving in Ends

With the wrong side of your piece facing you, thread tail end onto a tapestry needle and insert the needle underneath the posts of three or four stitches (**2**). Pull yarn through and snip close to the work (**3**). If you feel it necessary you can repeat this process by working back through the same stitches: skip the first stitch and then insert your needle underneath the next few stitches. Pull yarn through and snip yarn close to the work.

Joining the Yarn to Begin a Skirt, Dress, Ruffle or Collar

Some details that build the wardrobe of these characters, like skirts or ruffles, are crocheted to the body of the doll and are not removable. To achieve this the pattern will call for a special round where you will work into the remaining front loops in the body of your doll.

To join in the yarn to create a skirt or dress you will always need to hold your doll head down (even if the head is not quite finished) and look for the remaining front loop right in the middle of the back of your doll. I usually pick the last front loop of the round (which is next to the first front loop of the round) and join my yarn right there and then crochet towards the left (**4**).

Closing the Arms

The arms of the dolls look like crochet tubes and they do not need to be filled with stuffing. In the last round you will be asked to close the tube by flattening the opening, so that 4 stitches of the top layer become aligned with 4 stitches of the lower layer (**5**). Once you've achieved this, join both layers by crocheting 1 sc in each pair of stitches (**6**). You will end up with 4 sc (**7**). Fasten off but remember to leave a long yarn tail to sew to the body.

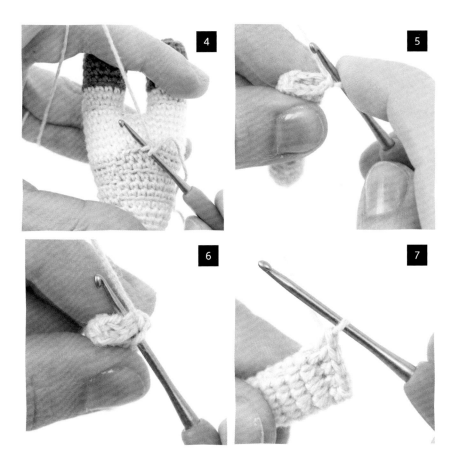

Sewing the Arms

Thread yarn tail onto a tapestry needle and place the arm against the side of the body. When you are happy with placement insert the needle through a stitch on the body (**1**), pull yarn through. Insert needle through the top of the next stitch on the arm (**2**), pull yarn through. Repeat this process until the arm is sewn in place (**3**). Secure yarn with a few stitches and follow the instructions for hiding the ends inside the doll.

TIP

I usually sew the arms to the dolls between rounds 28 and 29 of the body. But this is up to you. If the doll has a collar, remember to lift it slightly before sewing!

Crocheting Curls

Many of the dolls in this book have curls, some of them are short and some of them are longer. All of these curls start with a foundation chain (the length of which will be indicated in the pattern), working from the hair cap (**1**) and then you will have to crochet 1 sc in each back loop of each chain stitch (**2**) until you reach the edge of the hair piece again (**3**). Do not use the back bumps of the foundation chain unless specified. These hair locks will tend to curl naturally as you go, but if they don't, help them with your fingers, by twisting them into shape, as if they were old telephone cables.

Sewing the Hair

Use small straight stitches to sew the hair to the head, using the remaining yarn tail after fastening off. Work over the sc stitches of the hair (**4**) and making sure that you also work through the stitches of the head, to join them securely. You can space the stitches out because you don't need to work over every stitch (**5**). Don't pull yarn too tightly when sewing, otherwise your stitches may distort the shape of the head.

Sewing Loose Pieces

If required, stuff the piece to be sewn. Thread the tapestry needle and position the piece in place. Secure it with pins. Do you like it there? Then let's go! Using backstitching, sew the piece with the needle going under both loops of the last round.

TIP

If you want your curls to be thicker, you can crochet 2 sc into each chain stitch.

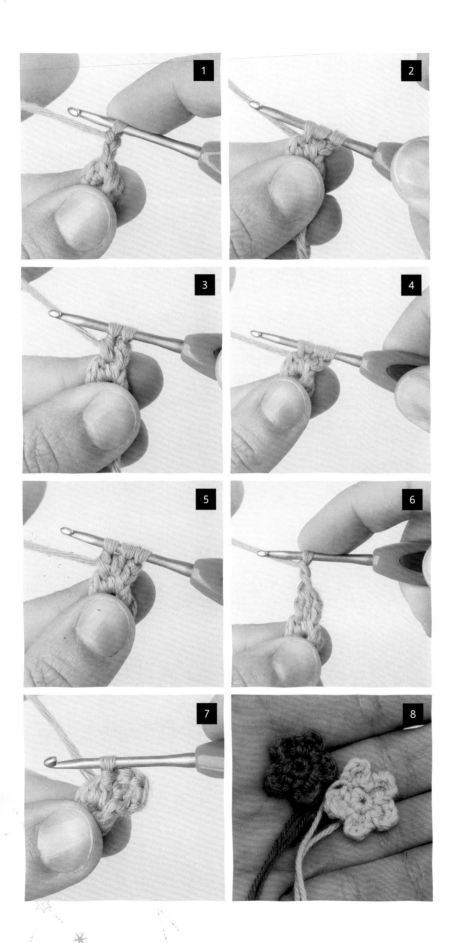

Flowers

For Virgo's flowers you will work the first round of 5 dc into a magic ring as instructed in the pattern.

Work one slip stitch in the next stitch, chain two (**1**).

Yarn over hook, insert the hook back into the same stitch, yarn over hook and pull yarn through the stitch (**2**).

Yarn over hook, pull yarn through two loops on your hook (**3**).

Yarn over hook, insert hook into the same stitch, yarn over hook and pull yarn through the stitch (**4**).

Yarn over hook, pull yarn through the first two loops on your hook (**5**).

Yarn over hook, pull yarn through the three remaining loops on your hook, chain two (**6**).

Work one slip stitch in the same stitch (**7**).

Repeat steps 1 to 7 a further 4 times to make 5 petals; finish with a slip stitch in the next stitch. Make as many flowers as instructed (**8**).

Inserting Wire Inside Certain Pieces

Some pieces, as Capricorn's horns or Scorpio's ponytail, carry a piece of wire inside to achieve a certain curvy effect. It's important to trim the wire to the desired length and to round the ends into tiny loops so they won't come out from inside the doll. Use round-nose pliers for this, a tool used in jewellery making. Of course, if you are planning on giving the doll to small child, avoid the use of wire altogether.

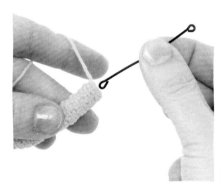

TIP

It is important to round the ends into tiny loops to ensure that the wire won't come out from inside the doll.

Pompoms

To make Leo's tiny pompoms, use a small fork and wind several rounds of yarn around its four tines. Break the yarn and tie a tight knot in the middle (leaving two tines to each side). Then cut the ends on both sides of the fork to create the pompom. Finally, trim the ends of yarn to achieve the desired size.

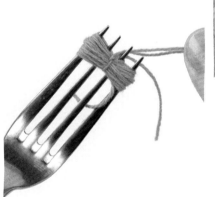

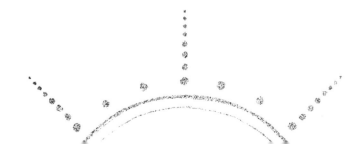

Aries

**Ideal best friend
Sagittarius**

**Ideal partner
Libra**

Taurus

**Ideal best friend
Virgo**

**Ideal Partner
Cancer**

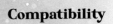

Gemini

**Ideal best friend
Aquarius**

**Ideal Partner
Sagittarius**

Cancer

**Ideal best friend
Taurus**

**Ideal Partner
Capricorn**

Leo

**Ideal best friend
Sagittarius**

**Ideal partner
Aries**

Virgo

**Ideal best friend
Gemini**

**Ideal Partner
Taurus**

Libra

**Ideal best friend
Leo**

**Ideal Partner
Gemini**

Scorpio

**Ideal best friend
Pisces**

**Ideal Partner
Cancer**

Sagittarius

Ideal best friend
Gemini

Ideal partner
Aries

Capricorn

Ideal best friend
Cancer

Ideal Partner
Aquarius

Aquarius

Ideal best friend
Libra

Ideal Partner
Virgo

Pisces

Ideal best friend
Taurus

Ideal Partner
Scorpio

About

Hello! I am Carla and I live in Buenos Aires, Argentina. I am 42, married and have two children (both boys, both red heads) and a dog.

In case you were wondering, I am a Virgo, which means that I am super organized, obsessed with details and a bit of a control-freak! Poor family of mine ... Nothing escapes my magnifying glass. Fortunately crochet has come to save me from my obsessions and making my stitches super extra tight has actually become my perfect way to decompress and channel my perfectionism (Is that a missed stitch? Yikes. Need to frog).

You might know me from my previous book, *Crochet Iconic Women*, which was also published by David and Charles, and it was a dream come true for me: a chance to honour an impressive line-up of women who offer daily inspiration for me. I hope you enjoy this new adventure as much as that one. I can't wait to see your makes!

Acknowledgements

Thank you so much my dear friends and followers for still supporting my designs and for joining me in this new journey!

Sarah Callard (Aries), my editor at David and Charles, words are not enough to thank you for placing your trust in me once again! It means the world to me. Honestly.

A million thanks to Lucy Waldron (Leo) for the magic she did in this book. She brought the stars and constellations to all these pages. Jason Jenkins (Aries), it was a pleasure to see you again and have your amazing photos in this new book. Sophie Seager (Aquarius), you rock! it's so much fun working with you! Thank you guys, for being so professional and taking care of me. It was amazing meeting you all in Exeter, UK and finally putting a face and a voice to all those emails and messages! You are family to me now!

Marie Owen-Smith (Cancer), you are such a thorough and detailed technical editor! I felt so safe in your hands! Thank you so very much! Jessica Cropper (Sagittarius), I truly appreciate how lovingly you took care of this project too. I am eternally grateful.

Thank you to my aunt Carine Mitrani (Leo), a true Astrologer still in the making (since she will never stop studying), for your guidance and suggestions in the descriptions of each Sun sign. To my family, yet again, thanks for your support and encouragement. You are my safety net. To my sister-in-law Celi (Leo), thanks for sharing with me this passion for the constellations, birth charts, stars and signs.

Finally, a huge thanks to my beloved husband (Taurus) and my beautiful boys (Gemini and Taurus) for being so patient with me, for accepting my absent-minded answers because I am mentally conceiving a design, for posing with my dolls, which you hate, and for interrupting whatever you are doing to "come take a photo of this step, please". I don't know what I would do without you!

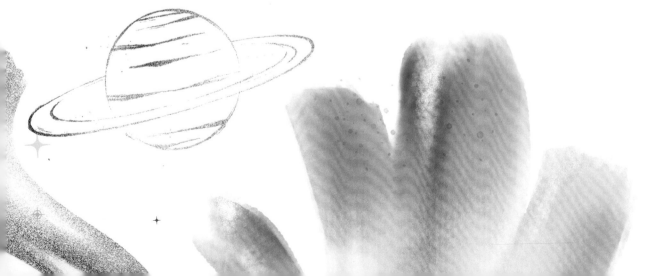

Index

A DAVID AND CHARLES BOOK
© David and Charles, Ltd 2022

David and Charles is an imprint of David and Charles, Ltd
Suite A, Tourism House, Pynes Hill, Exeter, EX2 5WS

Text and Designs © Carla Mitrani 2022
Layout and Photography © David and Charles, Ltd 2022

First published in the UK and USA in 2022

ISBN-13: 9781446309230 paperback
ISBN-13: 9781446381670 EPUB
ISBN-13: 9781446381663 PDF

This book has been printed on paper from approved suppliers
and made from pulp from sustainable sources.

Printed in the UK by Pureprint for:
David and Charles, Ltd
Suite A, Tourism House, Pynes Hill, Exeter, EX2 5WS

10 9 8 7 6 5 4 3 2 1

Publishing Director: Ame Verso
Senior Commissioning Editor: Sarah Callard
Managing Editor: Jeni Chown
Editor: Jessica Cropper
Project Editor: Marie Owen-Smith
Head of Design: Sam Staddon
Designers: Lucy Waldron and Blanche Williams
Pre-press Designer: Ali Stark
Photography: Jason Jenkins
Production Manager: Beverley Richardson

David and Charles publishes high-quality books on
a wide range of subjects. For more information visit
www.davidandcharles.com.

Share your makes with us on social media using #dandcbooks
and follow us on Facebook and Instagram by searching
for @dandcbooks.

Layout of the digital edition of this book may vary depending
on reader hardware and display settings.